Easy Piano

More Songs from glee

Music From The FOX Television Show

ISBN 978-1-61774-171-5

HAL•LEONARD® CORPORATION

7777 W. BLUEMOUND RD. P.O. BOX 13819 MILWAUKEE, WI 53213

Visit Hal Leonard Online at
www.halleonard.com

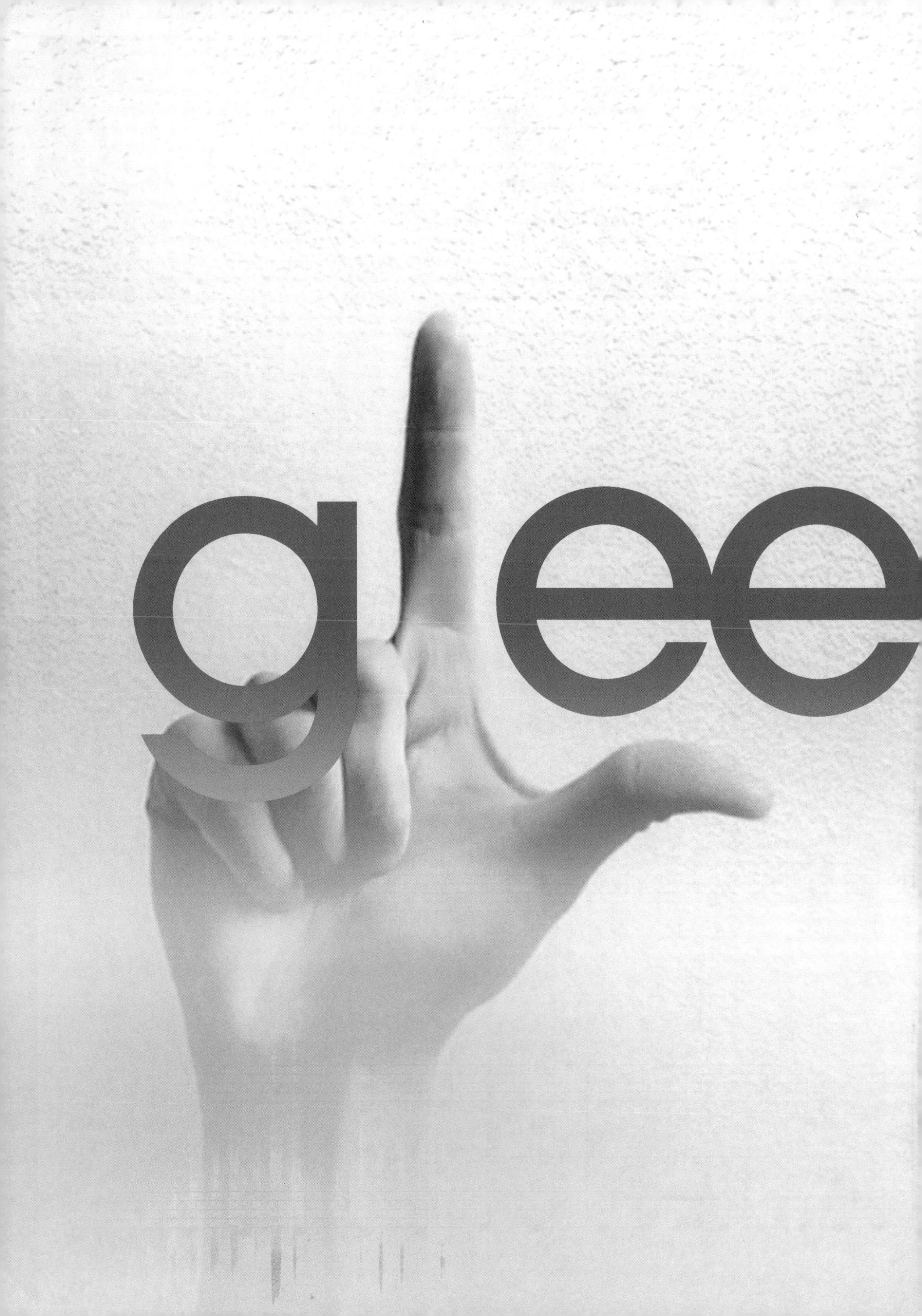
glee

AND I AM TELLING YOU
I'M NOT GOING

from DREAMGIRLS

Music by HENRY KRIEGER
Lyric by TOM EYEN

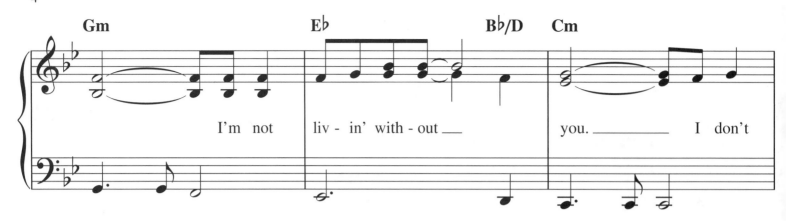

I'm not liv - in' with - out ___ you. ___ I don't

want to be free. ___ I'm stay - in', ___ I'm stay - in', and

you, and you, you're gon - na love ___ me. ___ Ooh, ___

___ you're gon - na love ___ me.

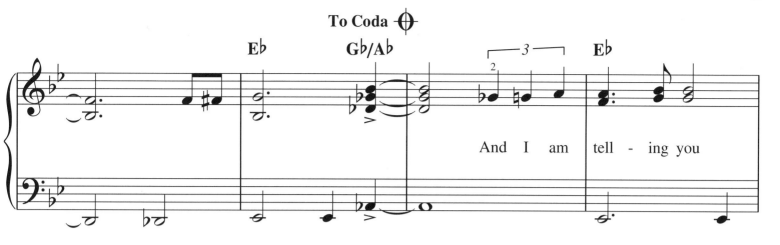

To Coda ⊕

Eᵇ   Gᵇ/Aᵇ   Eᵇ

And I am tell - ing you

F/Eᵇ   Dm7   Gm7   Gm/F

I'm   not   go - ing, __   e - ven though the rough

Eᵇ   Cm7   Eᵇ/F

times   are   show - ing.   There's _ just   no   way, __   there's

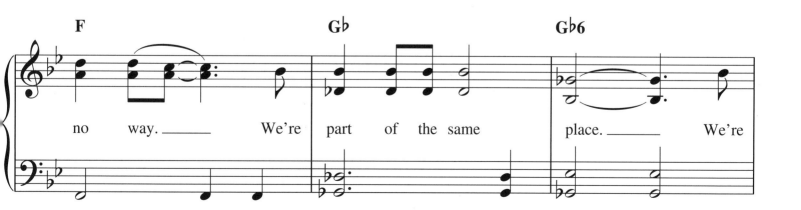

F   Gᵇ   Gᵇ6

no   way. _____   We're   part   of   the   same   place. _____   We're

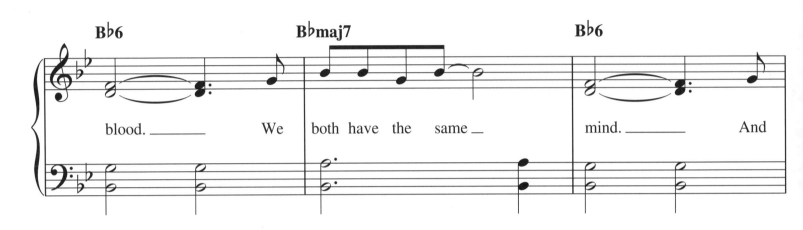

finding that there's no-bod-y there. _____ Dar-ling, there's

no way, no, no, no, no way I'm liv-in' with-

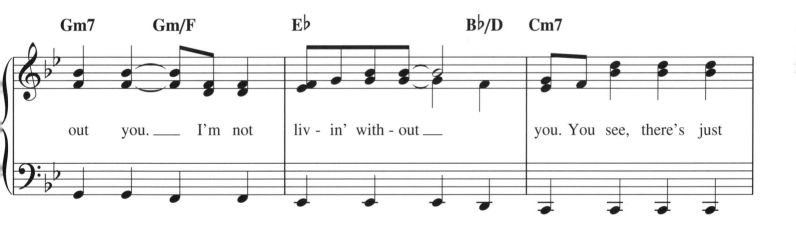

out you. ___ I'm not liv-in' with-out ___ you. You see, there's just

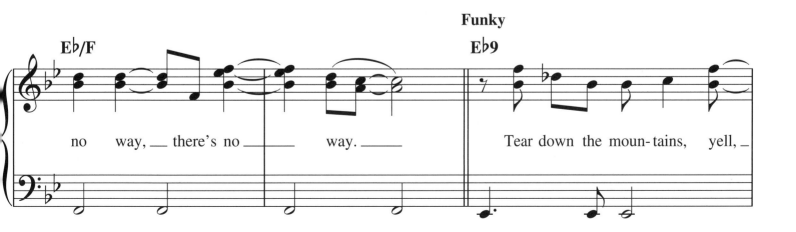

no way, ___ there's no _____ way. _____ Tear down the moun-tains, yell, _

scream and shout. You can say what you want, _ I'm not walk-in' out. ____

Stop all the riv - ers, push, strike and kill. I'm not gon - na leave _ you, there's

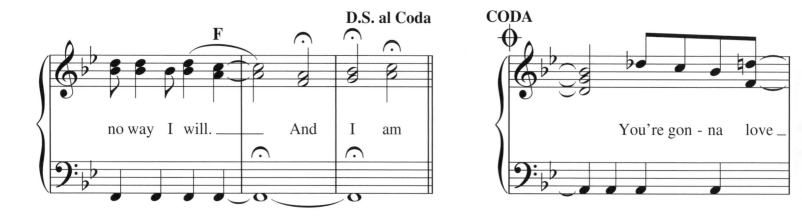

no way I will. ____ And I am

You're gon - na love _

____ me. ____ Yes, you are. Ooh, ooh, love me, ___

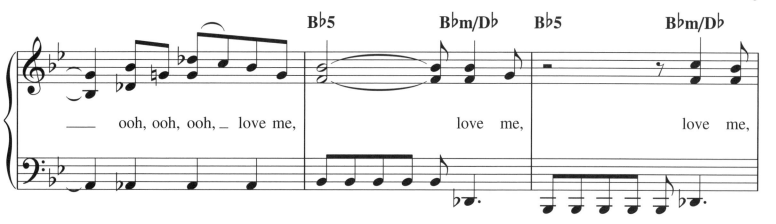

ooh, ooh, ooh, love me, love me, love me,

love me, love me.

You're gon-na love

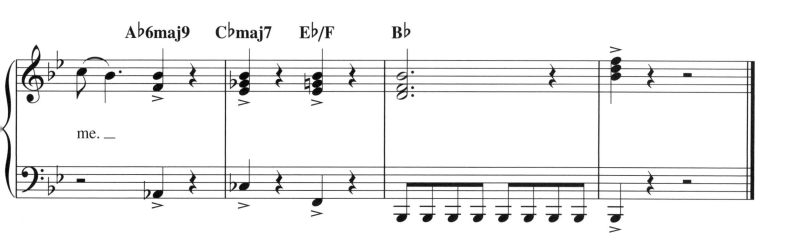

me.

ANY WAY YOU WANT IT/ LOVIN', TOUCHIN', SQUEEZIN'

Words and Music by STEVE PERRY
and NEAL SCHON

LOVIN', TOUCHIN', SQUEEZIN'
Words and Music by
STEVE PERRY

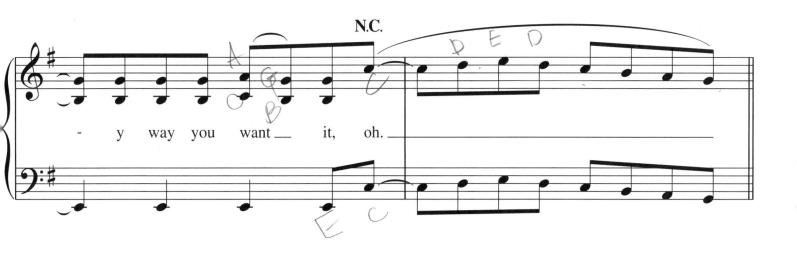

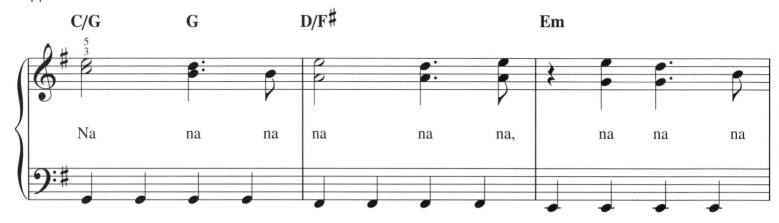

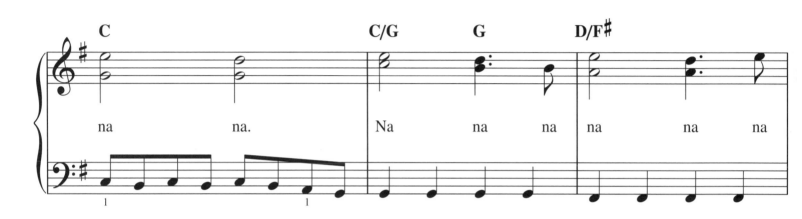

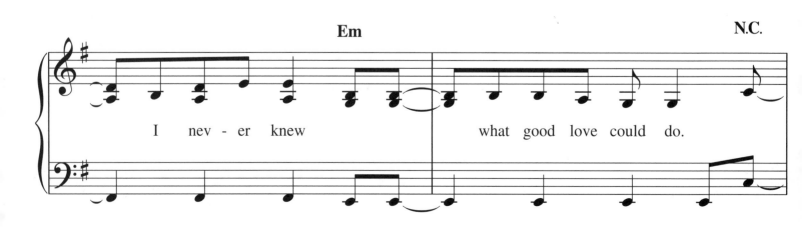

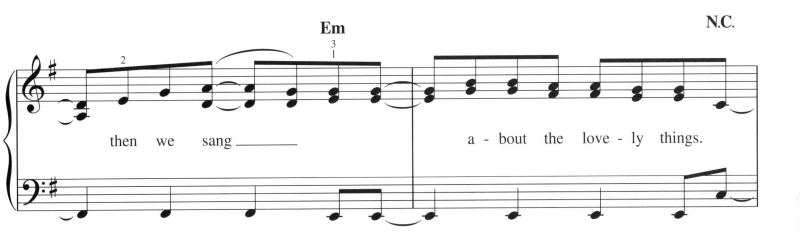

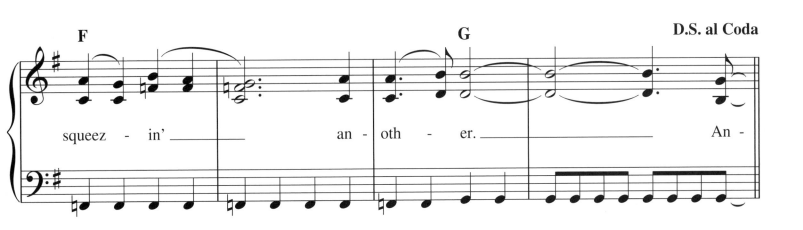

na. _____

Guitar solo

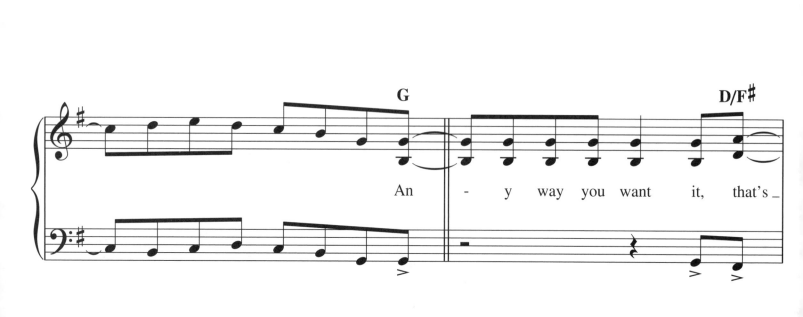

An - y way you want it, that's _

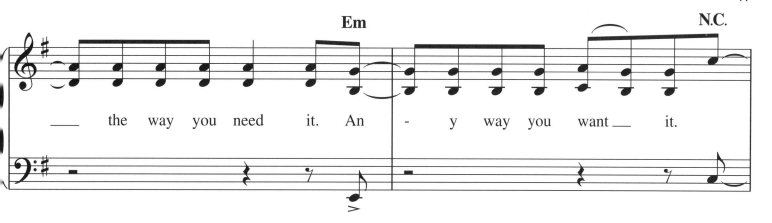

the way you need it. An - y way you want __ it.

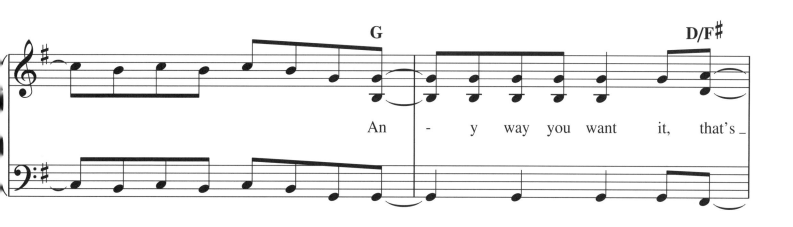

An - y way you want it, that's _

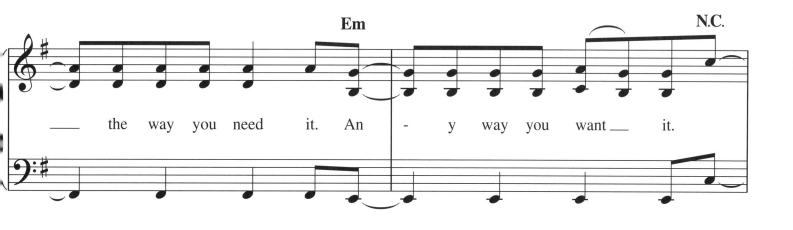

the way you need it. An - y way you want __ it.

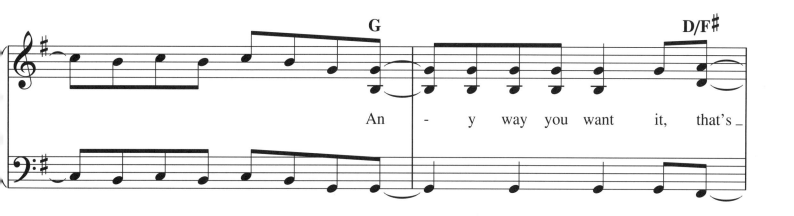

An - y way you want it, that's _

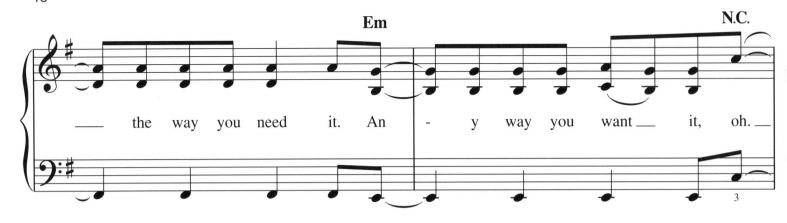

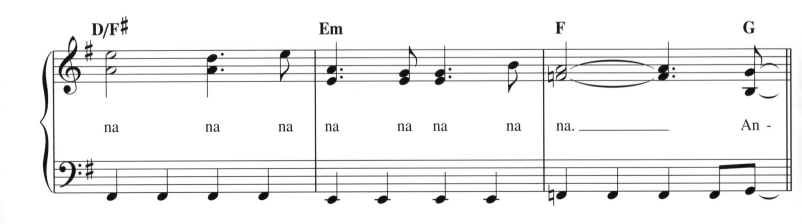

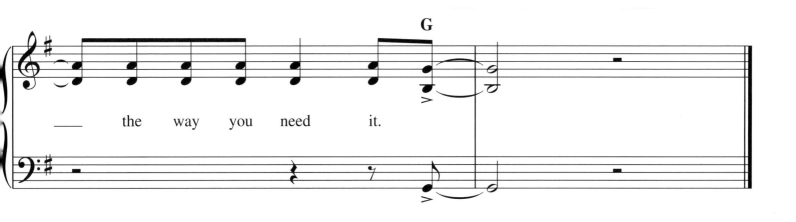

BOHEMIAN RHAPSODY

Words and Music by
FREDDIE MERCURY

Slowly, freely

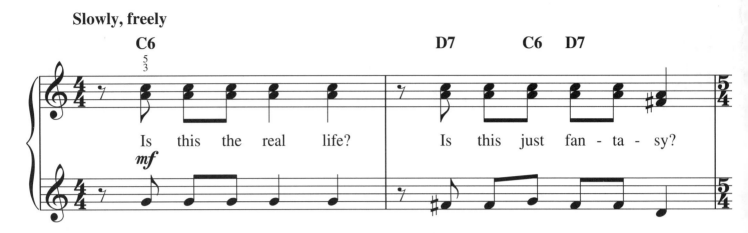

Is this the real life? Is this just fan - ta - sy?

Caught in a land - slide, no es - cape from re - al - i - ty.

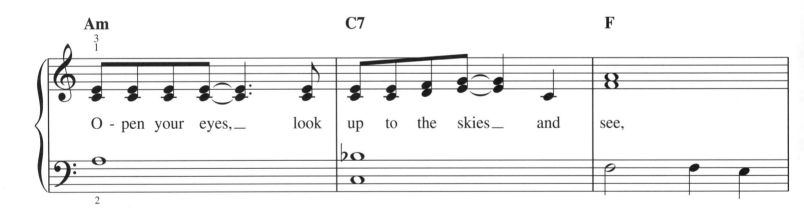

O - pen your eyes,__ look up to the skies__ and see,

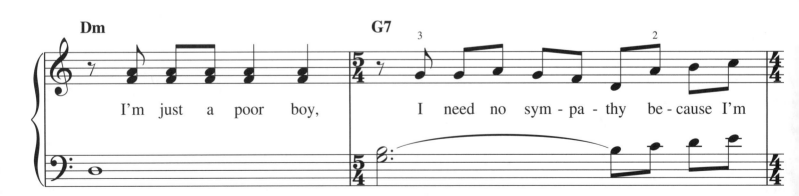

I'm just a poor boy, I need no sym - pa - thy be - cause I'm

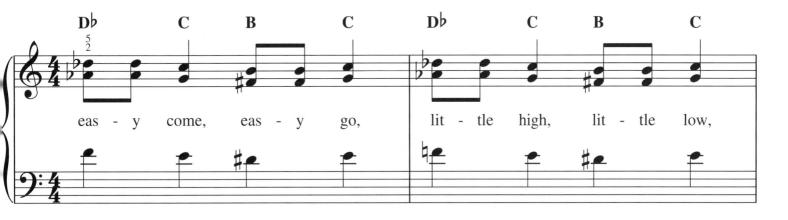

easy come, easy go, little high, little low,

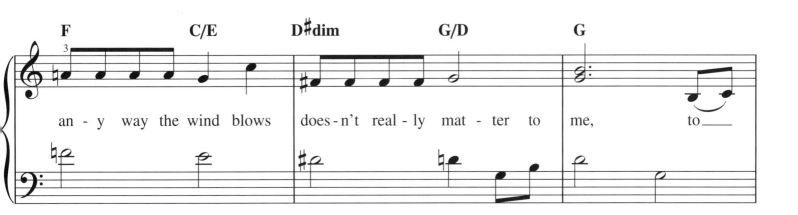

any way the wind blows doesn't really matter to me, to

me.

Slowly, steady tempo

Mama   just
Too late,   my

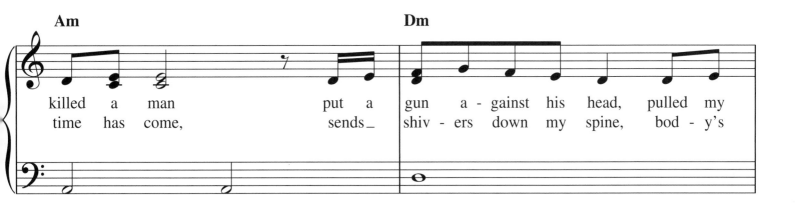

killed a man   put a   gun against his head, pulled my
time has come,   sends shivers down my spine, body's

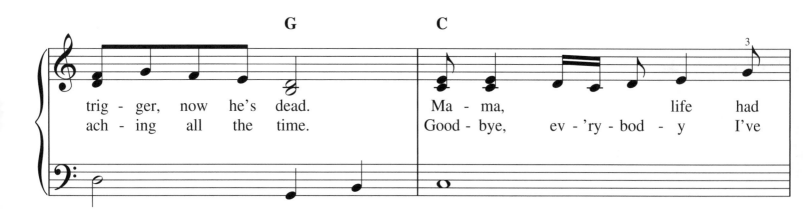

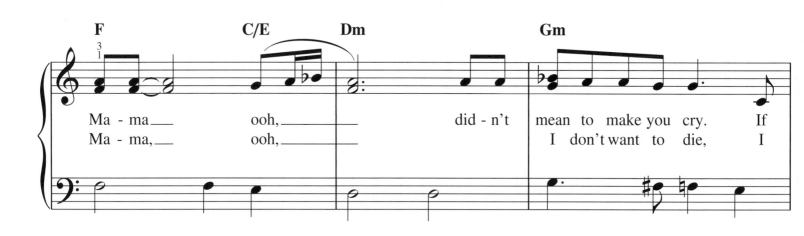

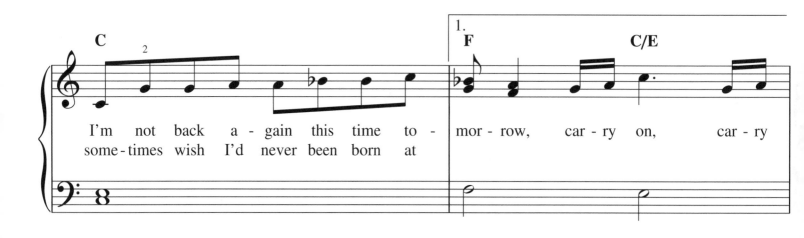

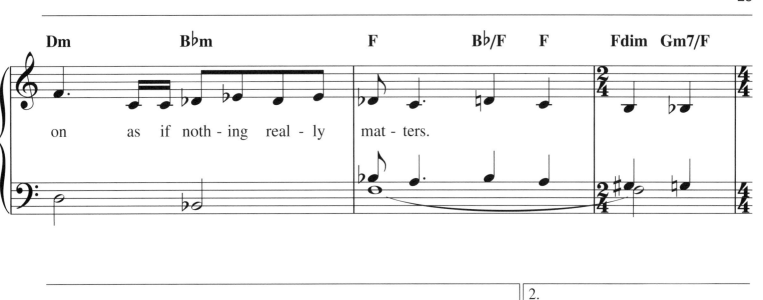

Dm **B♭m** **F** **B♭/F** **F** **Fdim** **Gm7/F**

on   as if noth - ing   real - ly   mat - ters.

C **2.** **F** **C/E**

all.

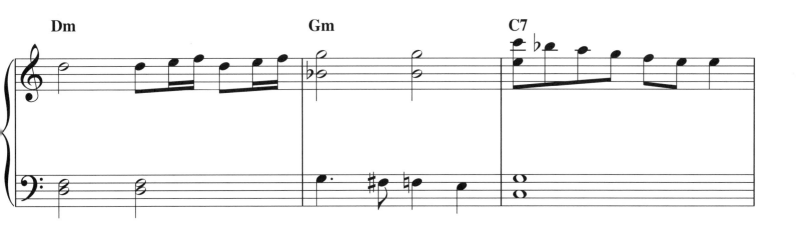

Dm **Gm** **C7**

F **Am/E** **Dm** **Gm**

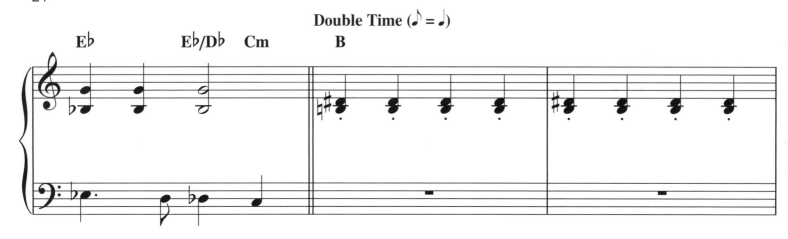

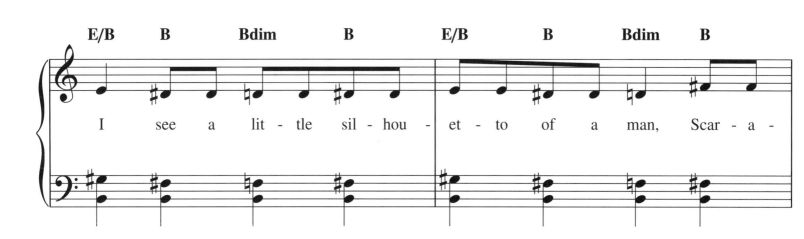

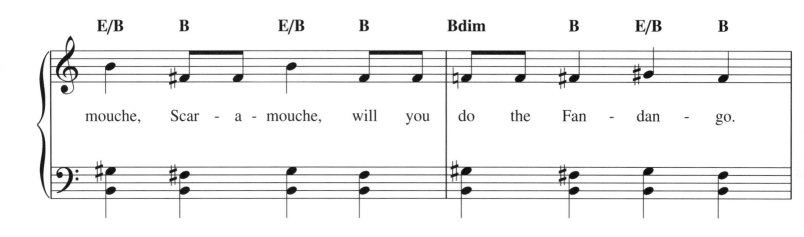

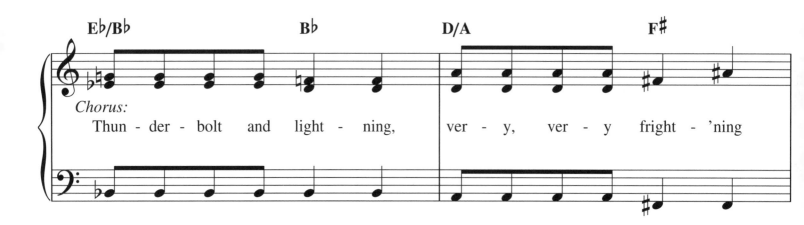

me. (Gal - li - le - o.) Gal - li - le - o. (Gal - li - le - o.) Gal - li -

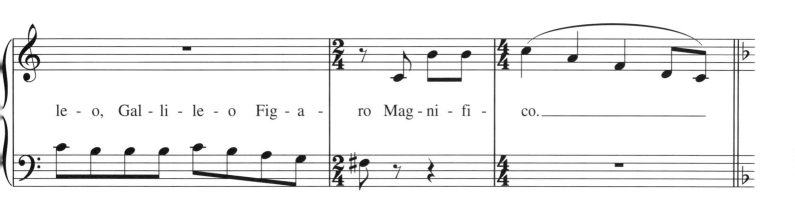

le - o, Gal - li - le - o Fig - a - ro Mag - ni - fi - co._____

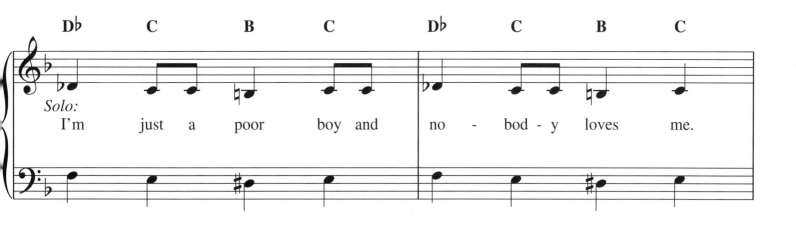

Solo:
I'm just a poor boy and no - bod - y loves me.

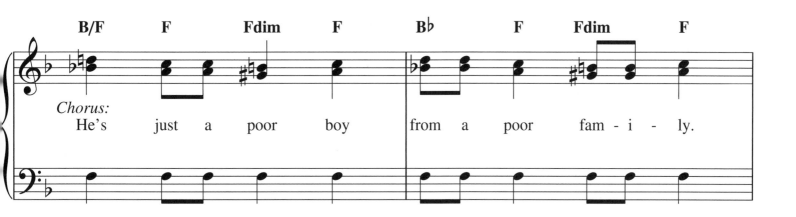

Chorus:
He's just a poor boy from a poor fam - i - ly.

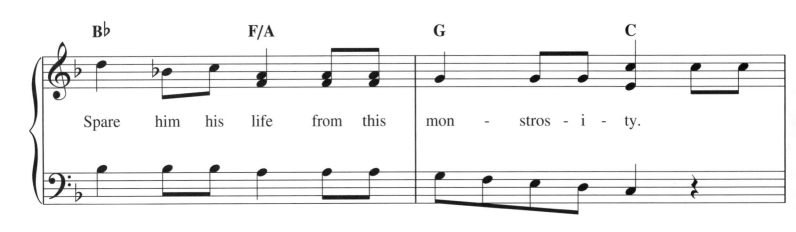

Spare him his life from this mon - stros - i - ty.

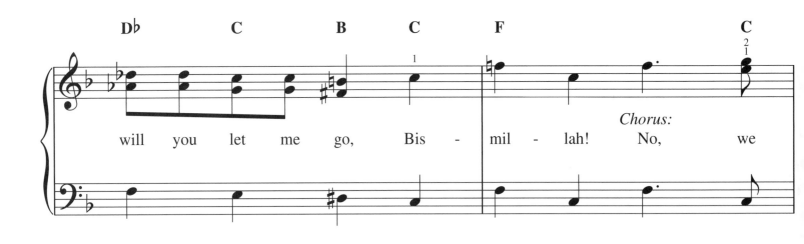

Solo:
Eas - y come, eas - y go,

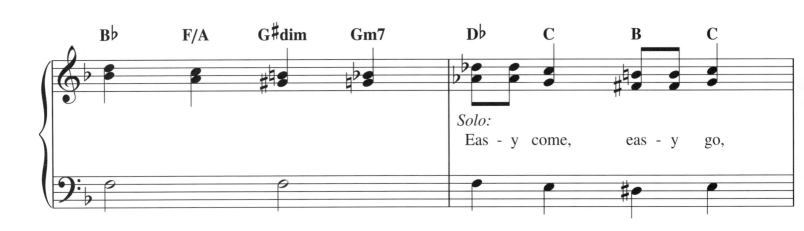

will you let me go, Bis - mil - lah! No, we

Chorus:

will not let you go. (Let him go!) Bis - mil - lah! We

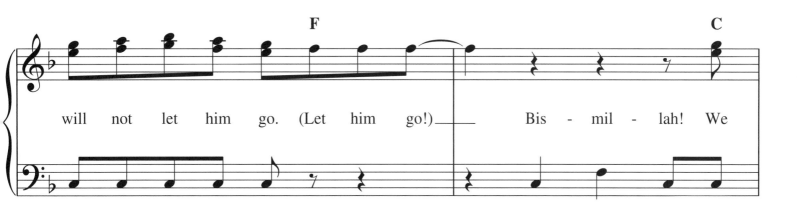

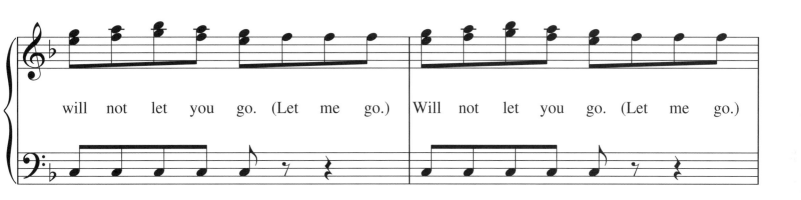

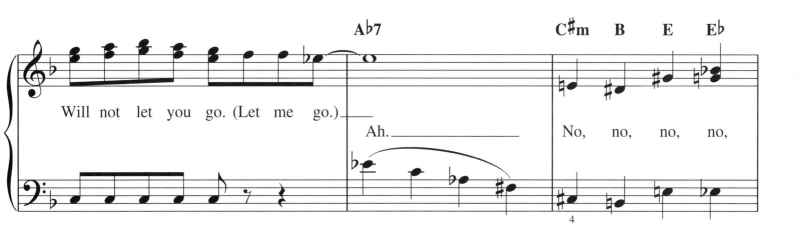

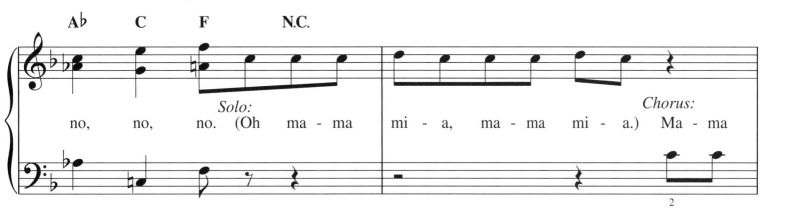

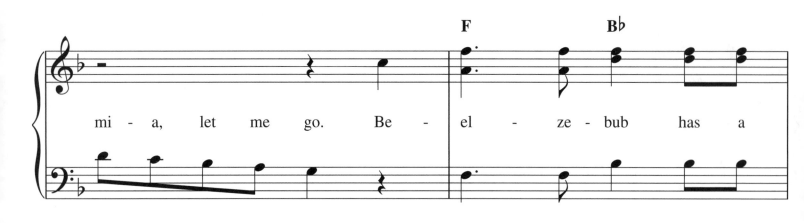

mi - a, let me go. Be - el - ze - bub has a

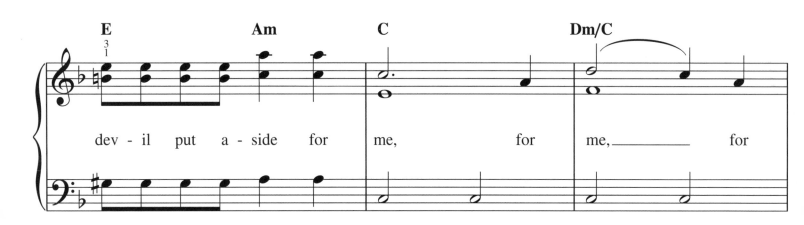

dev - il put a - side for me, for me,_____ for

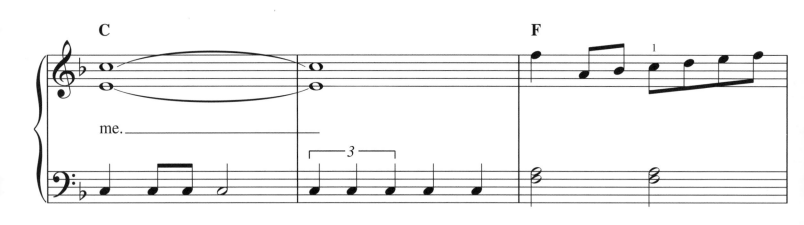

me._____

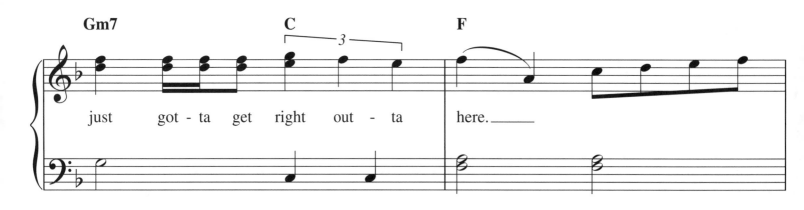

just got-ta get right out-ta here._____

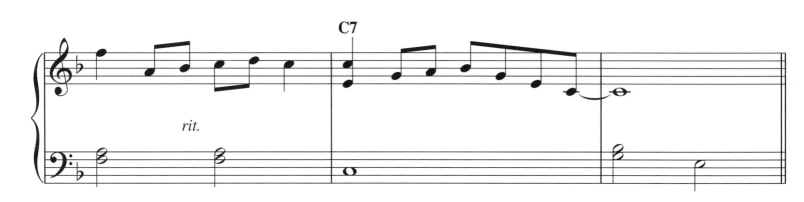

rit.

Slowly, a tempo

Noth-ing real-ly mat-ters,

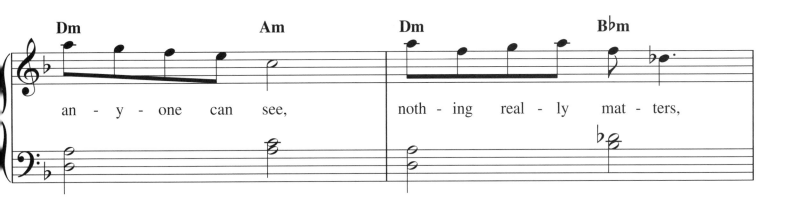

an - y - one can see, noth - ing real - ly mat - ters,

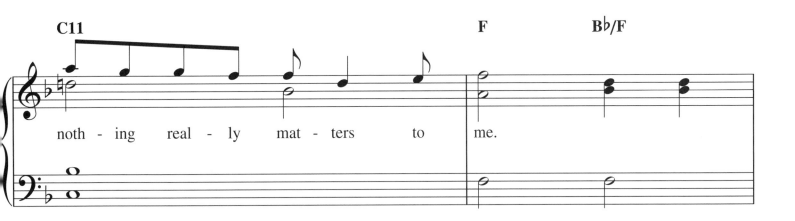

noth - ing real - ly mat - ters to me.

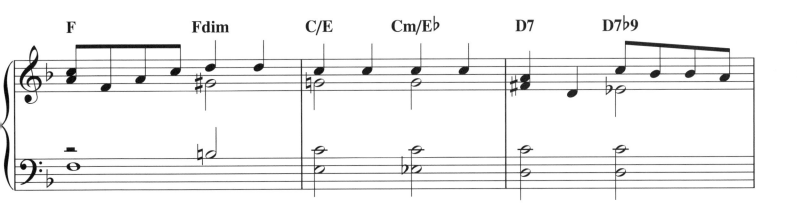

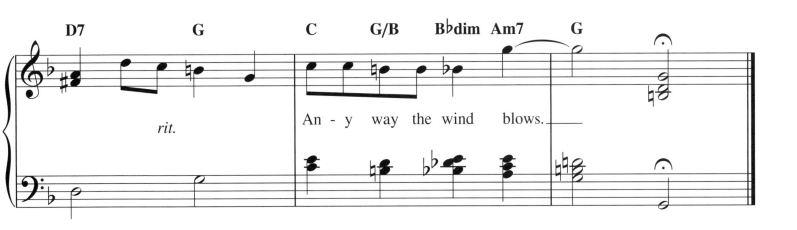

rit.

An - y way the wind blows.

BUST YOUR WINDOWS

Words and Music by JAZMINE SULLIVAN,
SALAAM REMI and DeANDRE WAY

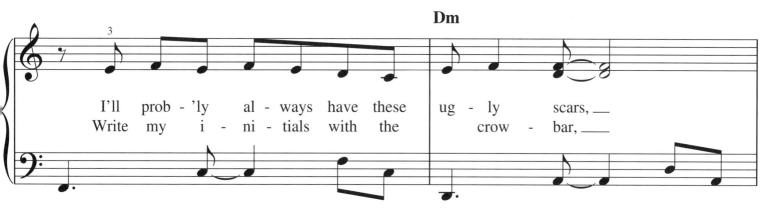

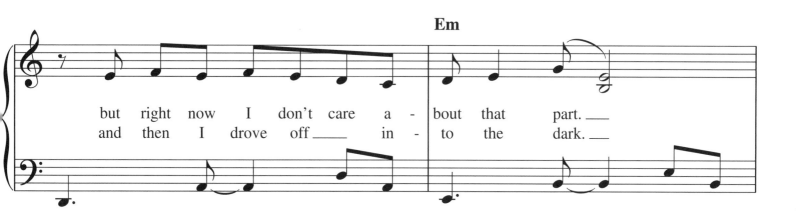

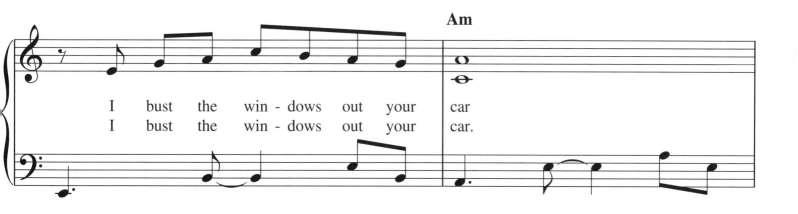

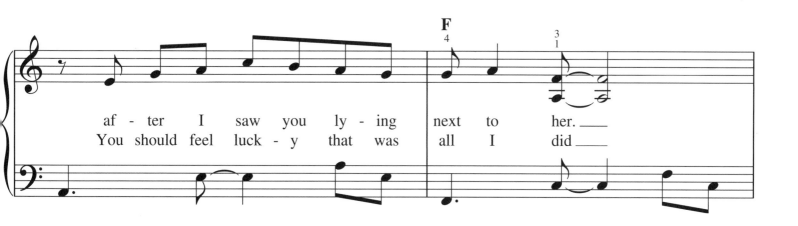

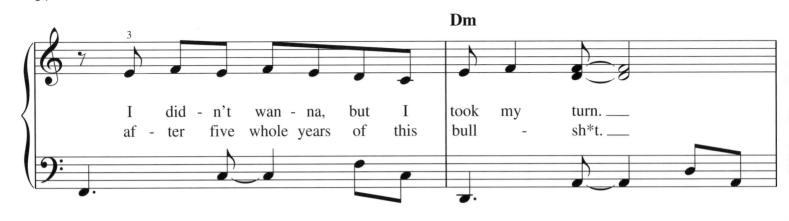

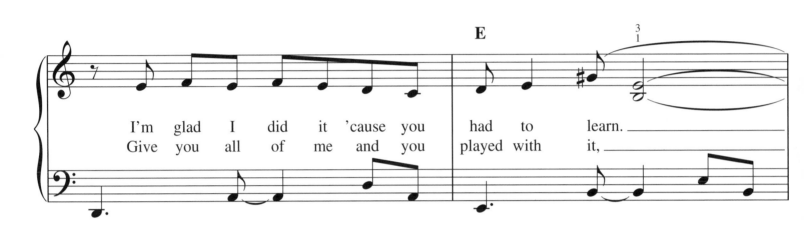

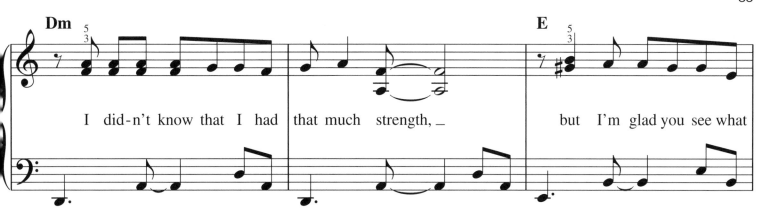

I did-n't know that I had that much strength, _ but I'm glad you see what

hap - pens when. _____ You see, you can't just play with

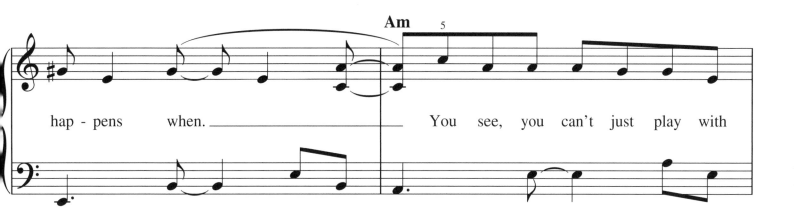

peo-ple's feel - ings, tell then you love them and don't mean _ it.

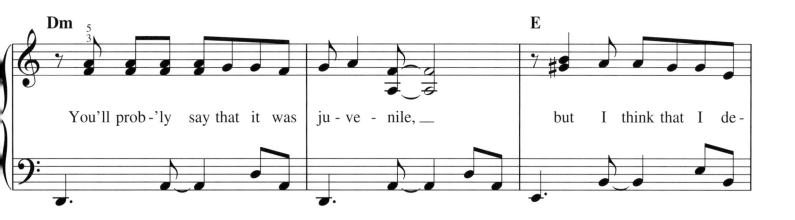

You'll prob -'ly say that it was ju - ve - nile, _ but I think that I de-

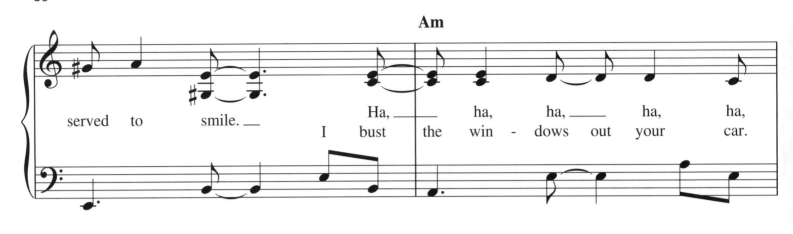

served to smile. ___ Ha, ___ ha, ha, ___ ha, ha,
I bust the win - dows out your car.

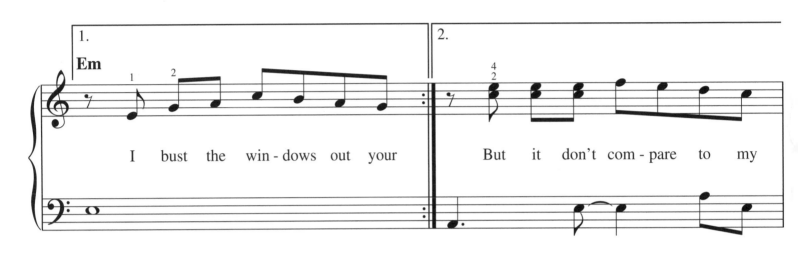

1.
I bust the win - dows out your

2.
But it don't com - pare to my

bro - ken heart. ___
You could nev - er feel how I

felt that day. ___
Un - til that hap - pens, ba - by,

you don't know pain. ___ No, ___ oh, ___

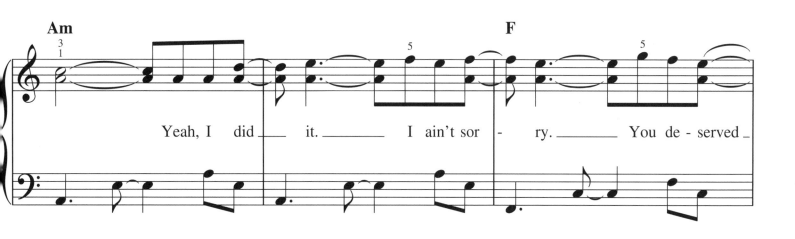

Yeah, I did ___ it. ___ I ain't sor - ry. ___ You de - served ___

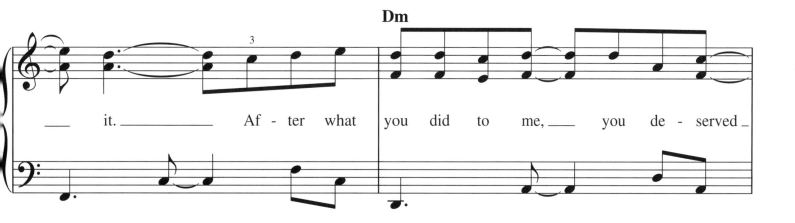

___ it. ___ Af - ter what you did to me, ___ you de - served ___

___ it. ___ I ain't sor - ry, ___ no, ___ no, ___ ooh. ___

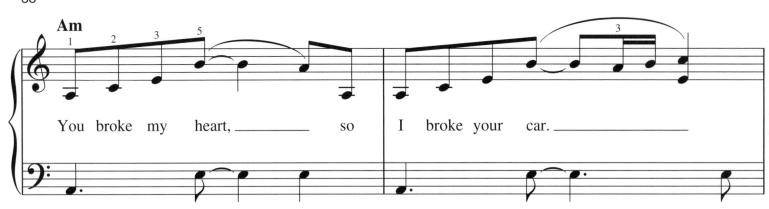

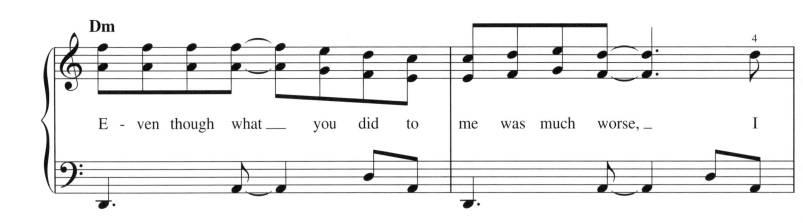

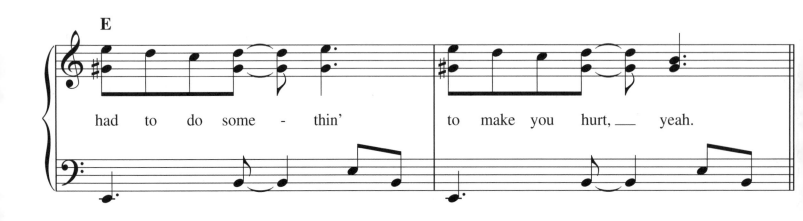

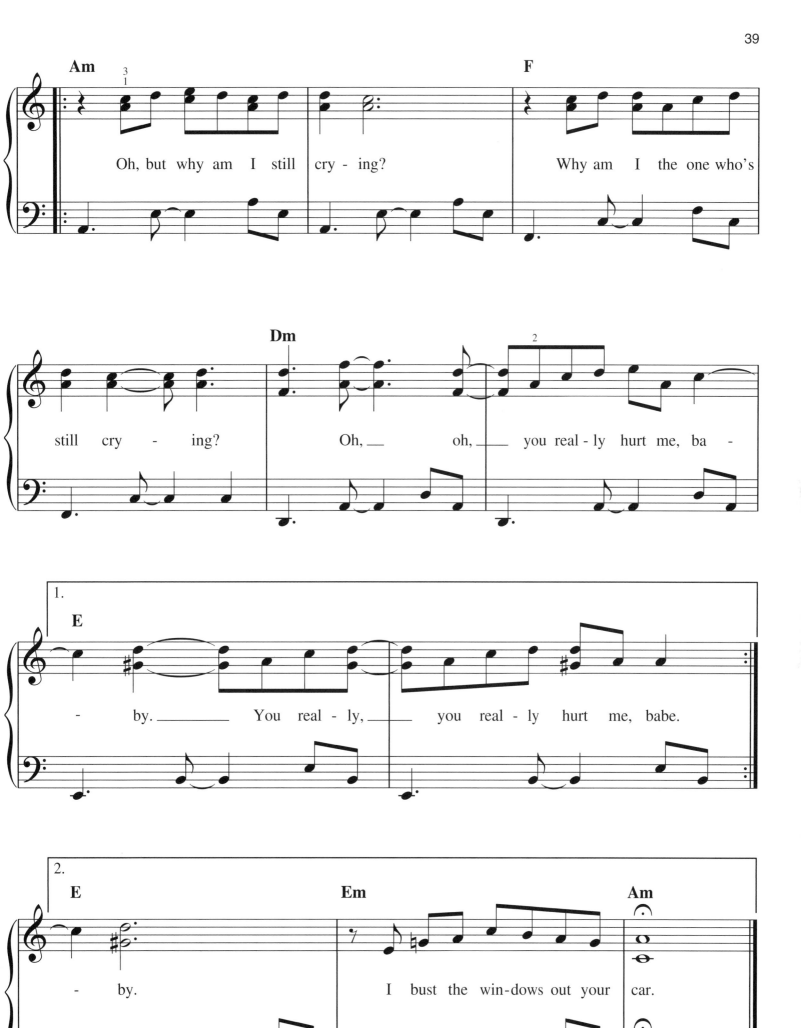

DANCING WITH MYSELF

Words and Music by BILLY IDOL
and TONY JAMES

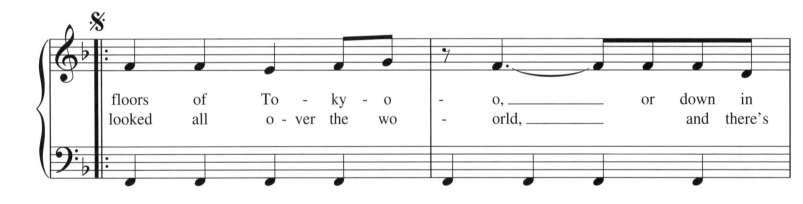

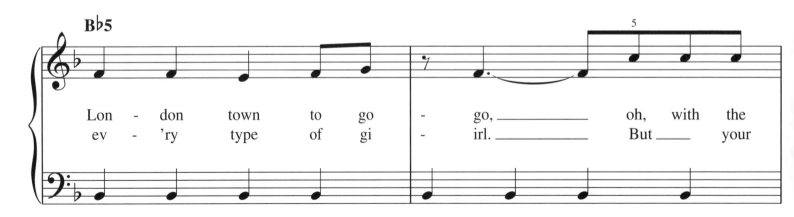

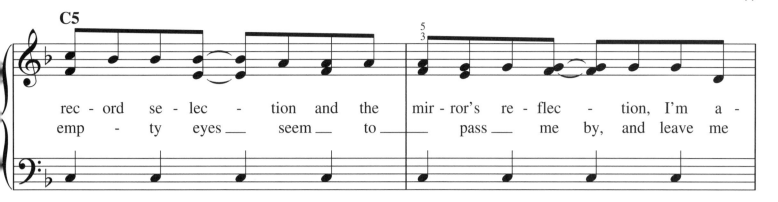

C5

rec - ord se - lec - tion and the | mir - ror's re - flec - tion, I'm a -
emp - ty eyes ___ seem ___ to ___ | pass ___ me by, and leave me

Bb5   **F5**

danc - in' with my - se - elf. _____ Oh, when there's | no one else in si -
danc - in' with my - se - elf. _____ So let's | sink an - oth - er dri -

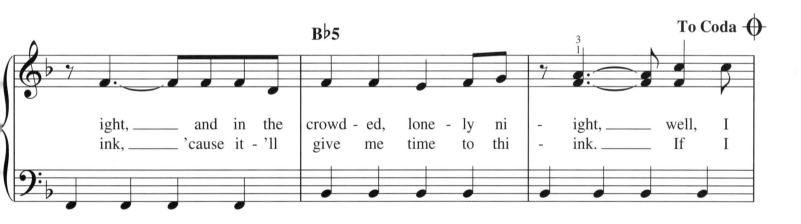

Bb5   **To Coda** ⊕

ight, _____ and in the | crowd - ed, lone - ly ni - ight, _____ well, I
ink, _____ 'cause it - 'll | give me time to thi - ink. _____ If I

C5

wait so long ___ for my | love vi - bra - tion, and I'm
had the chance, ___ I'd ask the | world to dance, ___ and I'd be

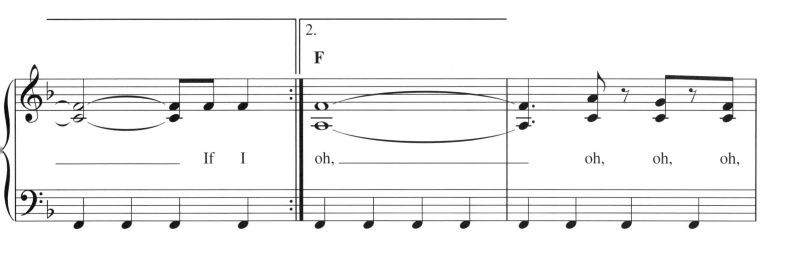

If I oh, oh, oh, oh,

oh, oh. Oh, oh, oh, oh,

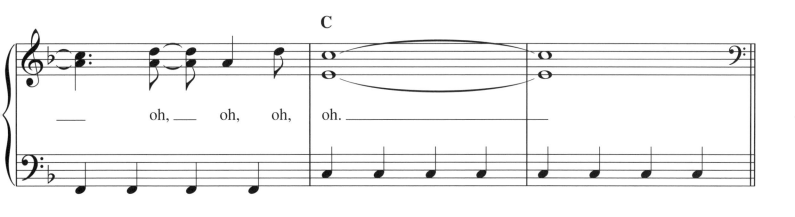

oh, oh, oh, oh.

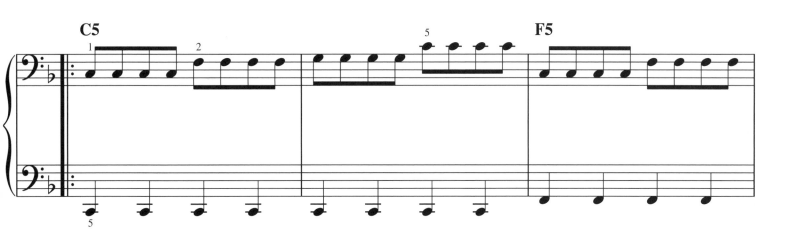

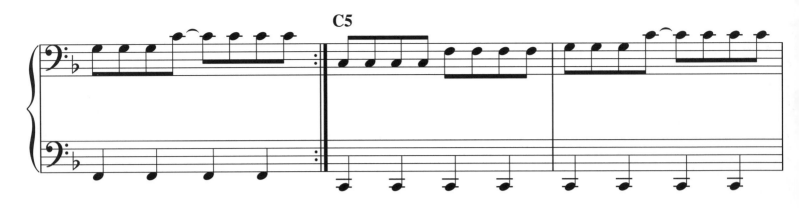

elf. Oh, oh, oh, danc - in' with my - se - elf. If I

had ___ the chance, _ I'd ask the world _ to dance, _ and if I

had ___ the chance, _ I'd ask the world __ to dance, _ if I

had ___ the chance, _ I'd ask the world __ to dance. _____

ENDLESS LOVE

Words and Music by
LIONEL RICHIE

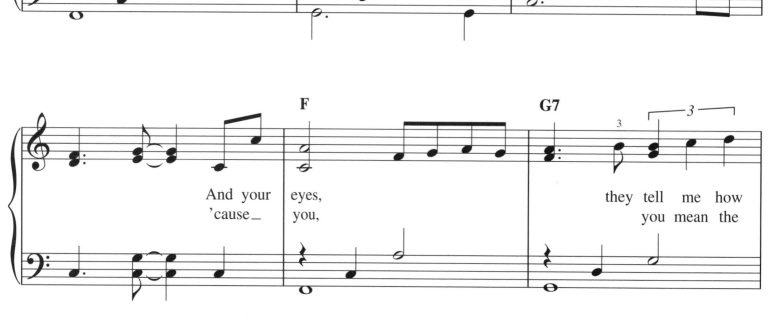

much   you   care.   Oh_____   yes,   you will
world   to   me.   Oh,__ I   know   I____

al - ways   be   my   end - less
found   in   you   my   end - less

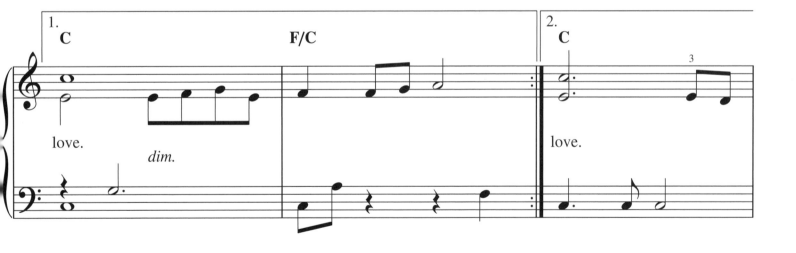

love.   *dim.*   love.

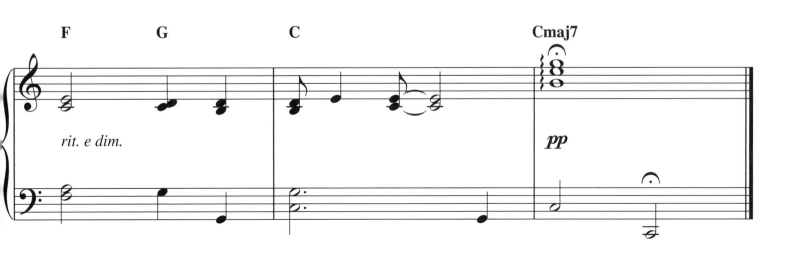

rit. e dim.   **pp**

FAITHFULLY

Words and Music by
JONATHAN CAIN

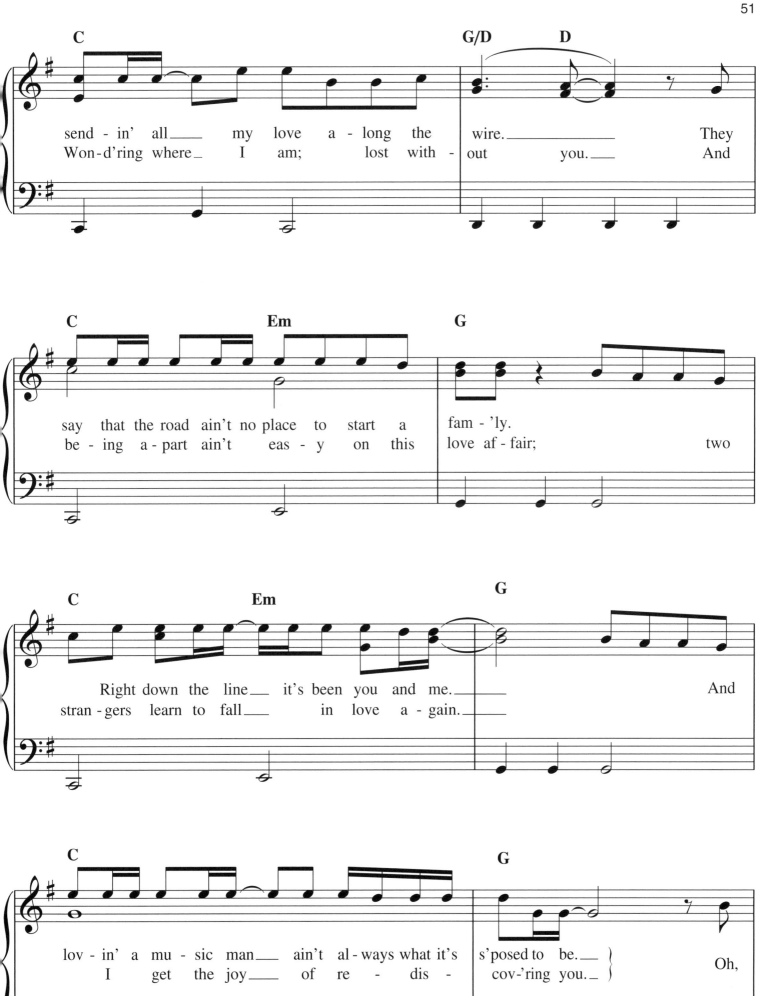

girl, you stand_ by me. I'm for - ev - er yours,_____

faith - ful - ly._____

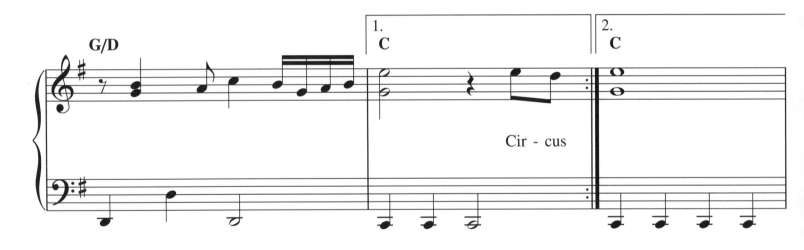

Cir - cus

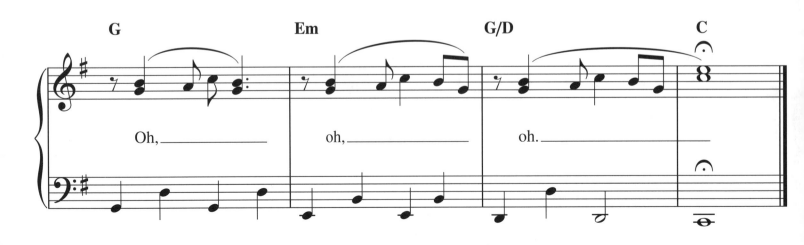

Oh,_____ oh,_____ oh.____

SMILE

Words and Music by LILY ALLEN,
IYIOLA BABALOLA, DARREN LEWIS,
CLEMENT DODD and JACKIE MITTOO

When you first left me, ___ I was want - ing more, ___ but you were kiss-ing that
ev - er you see me, ___ you say that you want me back ___ and I tell you it

girl next door; ___ what'd you do that for? ___
don't mean jack; ___ no, it don't mean jack. I

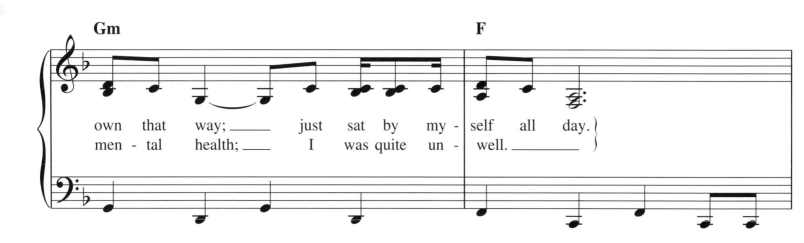

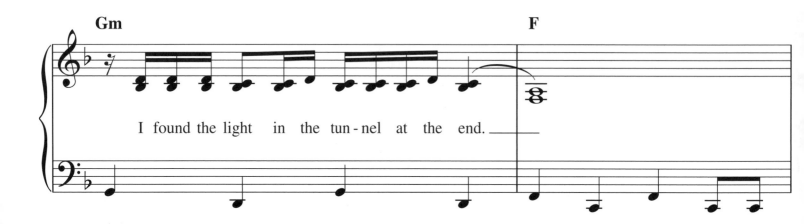

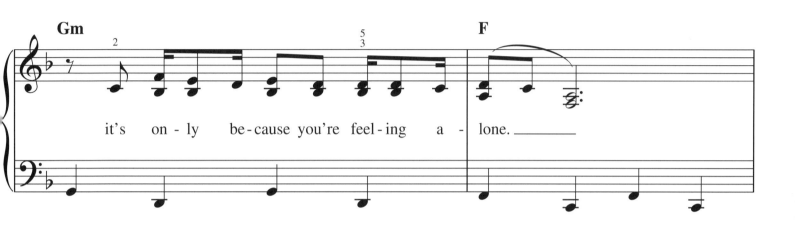

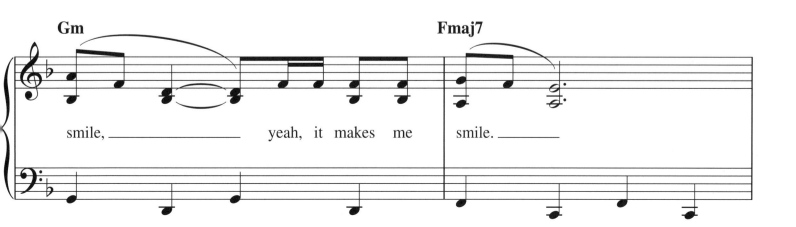

Gm

Fmaj7

At worst, ___ I feel bad for a - while, _____ but then I just

Gm

1. **Fmaj7**

smile; _____ I go a - head and smile. _____ When-

2.

Fmaj7

Gm

smile. _____ La la la la la la la la la la la la la la

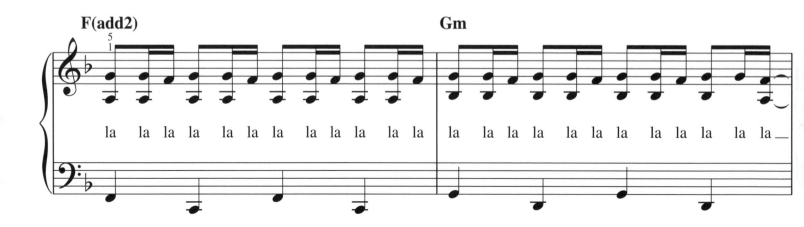

F(add2)

Gm

la la la la la la la la la la la la la la la la la la la la la la la la _

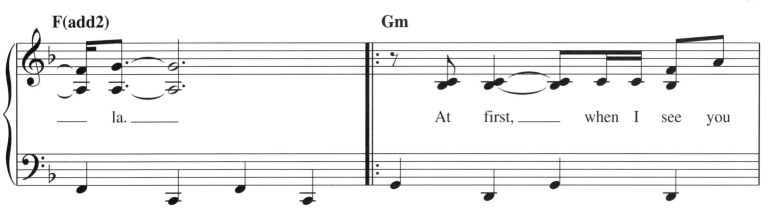

F(add2) · **Gm**

la. · At first, _____ when I see you

Fmaj7 · **Gm** · **F**

cry, _____ it makes me · smile, _____ yeah, it makes me · smile. ___

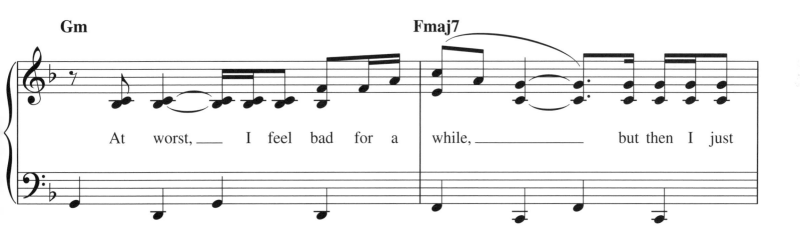

Gm · **Fmaj7**

At worst, ___ I feel bad for a · while, _____ but then I just

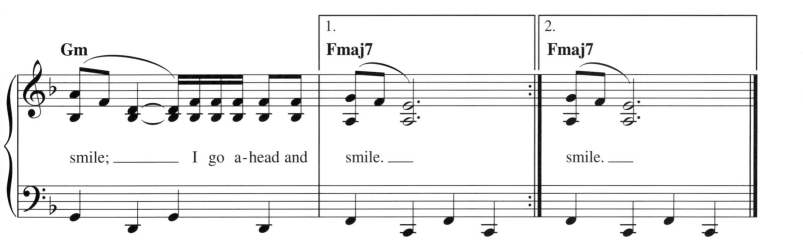

Gm · 1. **Fmaj7** · 2. **Fmaj7**

smile; _____ I go a-head and · smile. ___ · smile. ___

GOLD DIGGER

Words and Music by KANYE WEST,
RAY CHARLES and RENALD RICHARD

Moderately slow
N.C.

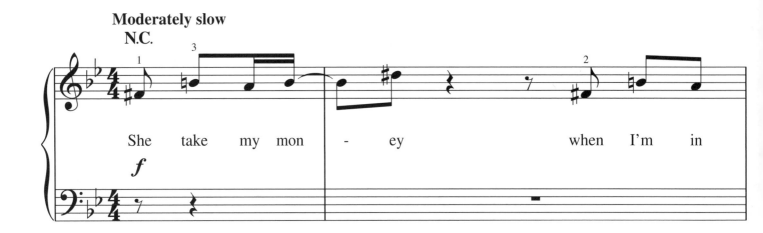

She take my mon - ey when I'm in

need. _____ Yeah, she's a trif - lin' friend in -

deed. _____ Oh, she's a gold dig - ger way o - ver

town, _____ that digs on me. She give me mon-

-ey _____ when I'm in need.
Rap: Now I ain't sayin' she's a gold digger,

She give me mon-
but she ain't messin' wit no broke, broke.

-ey when I'm in need.
Now I ain't sayin' she's a gold digger,

I got - ta
but she ain't messin' wit no broke, broke.

leave. I got - ta
Get down, girl, go 'head get down.

leave. I got - ta
Get down, girl, go 'head get down.

To Coda ⊕

leave.   I go-ta   leave.   Yeah, she give me mon-
Get down, girl, go 'head get down.   *Get down, girl, go 'head.*

B♭7

-ey _____ when I'm in need. _____   She give me mon-
Cutie da bomb, met her at a beauty salon with a baby Louis Vuitton under her underarms.   She said,

-ey _____ when I'm in need. _____   I got-ta
"I can tell you rock. I can tell ya by ya charm. Far as girls, you got a flock. I can tell by ya charm and ya arm."

E♭   **D.S. al Coda**

leave. _____   No, __ we ain't seen her!   She give me mon-
But I'm lookin' for the one. Have you seen her?

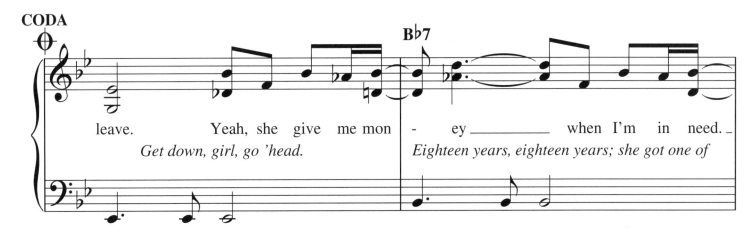

CODA

leave.   Yeah, she give me mon - ey _____ when I'm in need. _
Get down, girl, go 'head.   *Eighteen years, eighteen years; she got one of*

_____ She give me mon - ey _____ when I'm in need. _
you kids, got you for eighteen years.   *I know somebody payin' child support for one of these kids.*

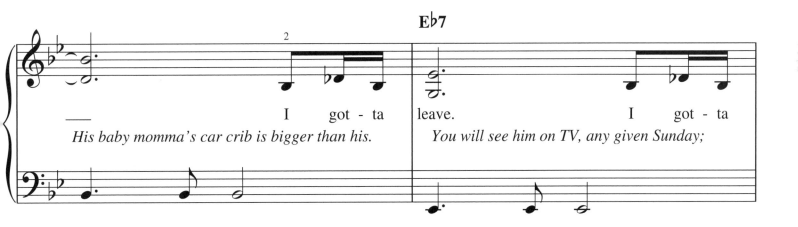

_ I got - ta leave.   I got - ta
His baby momma's car crib is bigger than his.   *You will see him on TV, any given Sunday;*

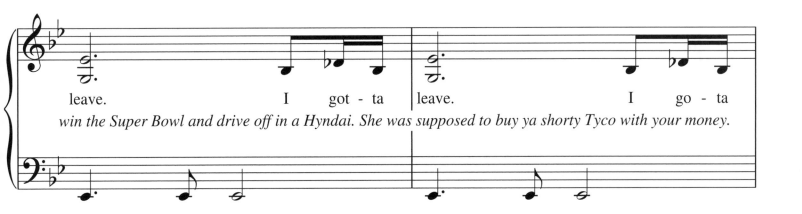

leave.   I got - ta leave.   I go - ta
win the Super Bowl and drive off in a Hyndai. She was supposed to buy ya shorty Tyco with your money.

Bb7

leave.   Yeah, she give me mon - ey _____ when I'm in need. _

She went to the doctor, got lipo with your money. She walk-in' 'round lookin' like Michael with your money.

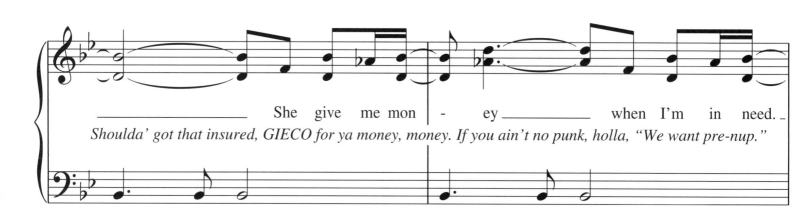

_____ She give me mon - ey _____ when I'm in need. _

Shoulda' got that insured, GIECO for ya money, money. If you ain't no punk, holla, "We want pre-nup."

N.C.

_ We want pre - nup!   Yeah!   She give me mon-

Bb7

- ey _____ when I'm in need. _____ She give me mon-

Now I ain't sayin' she's a gold digger,   *but she ain't messin' wit no broke, broke.*

HATE ON ME

Words and Music by JILL SCOTT,
ADAM BLACKSTONE and STEVEN McKIE

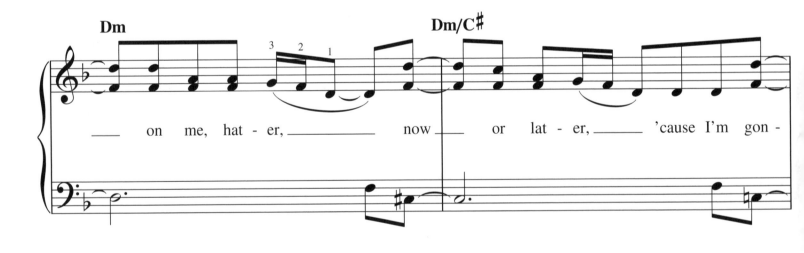

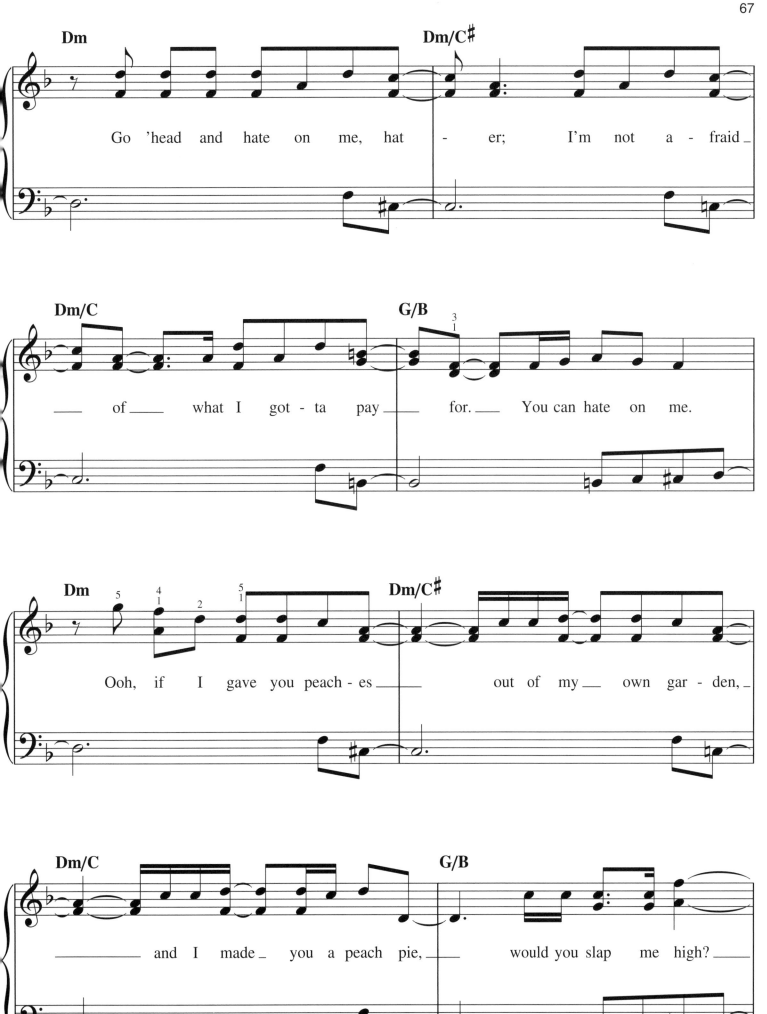

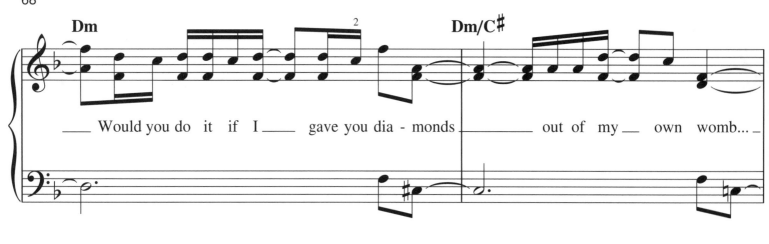

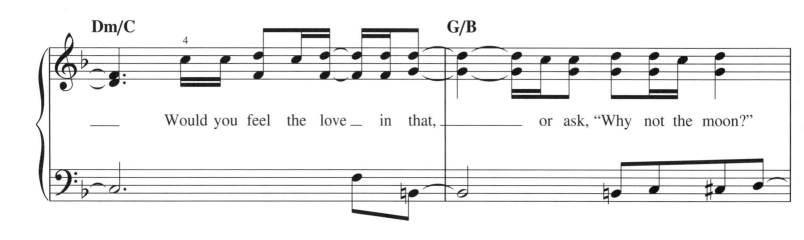

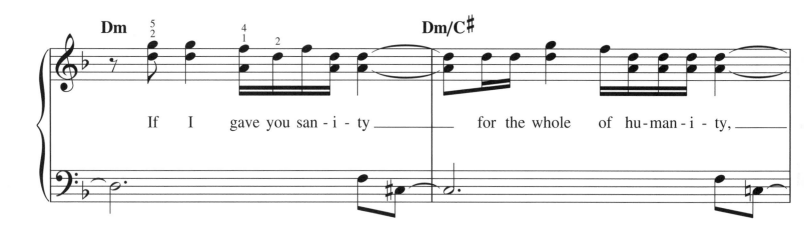

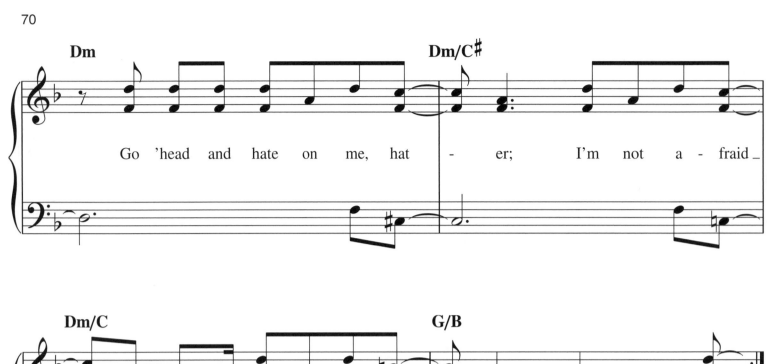

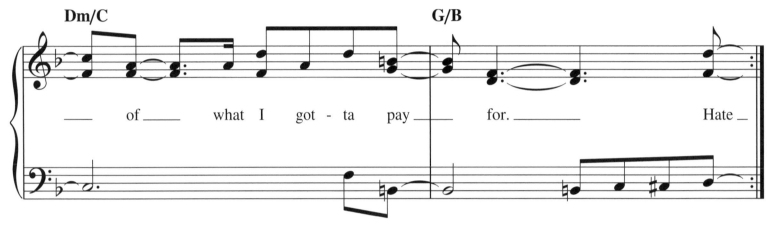

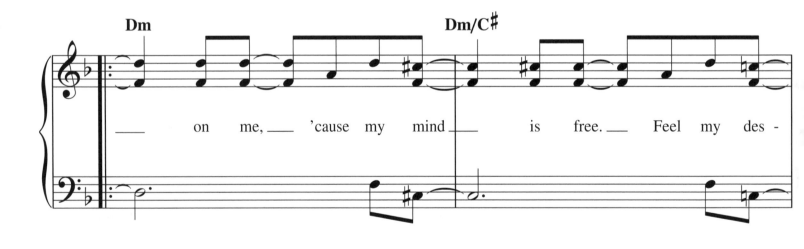

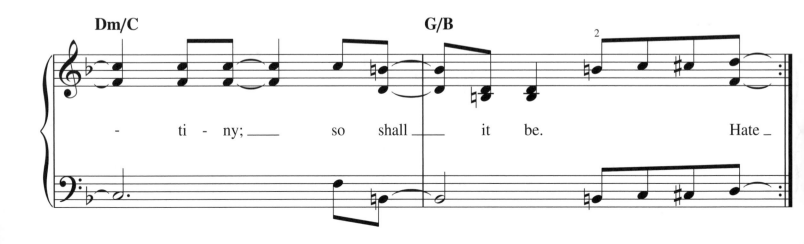

JUMP

Words and Music by DAVID LEE ROTH, EDWARD VAN HALEN,
ALEX VAN HALEN and MICHAEL ANTHONY

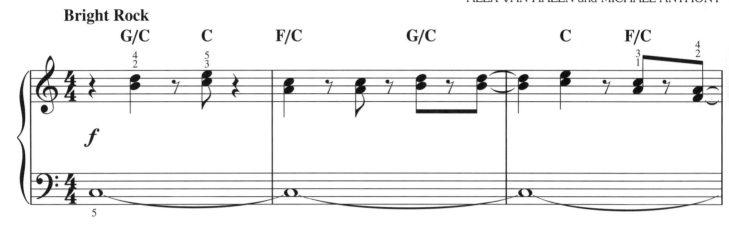

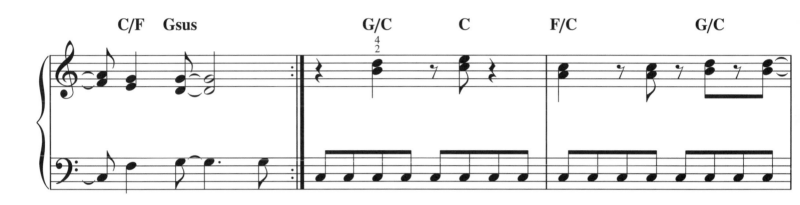

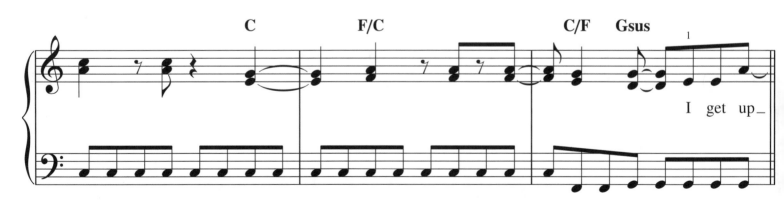

I get up

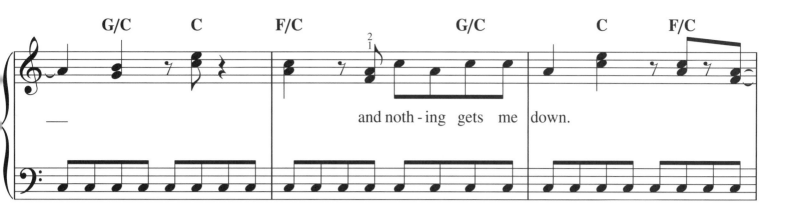

and noth-ing gets me down.

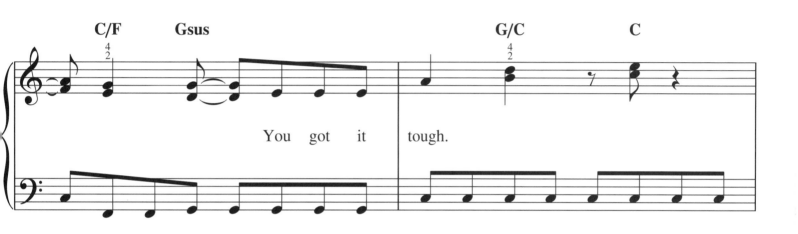

You got it tough.

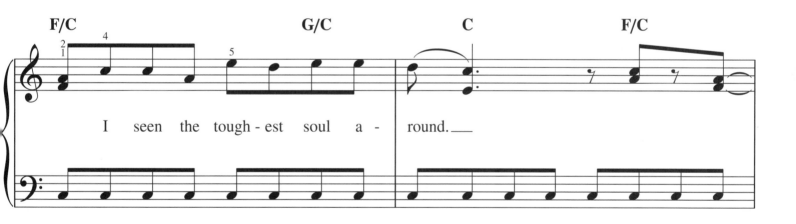

I seen the tough-est soul a - round.___

And I know,

know,

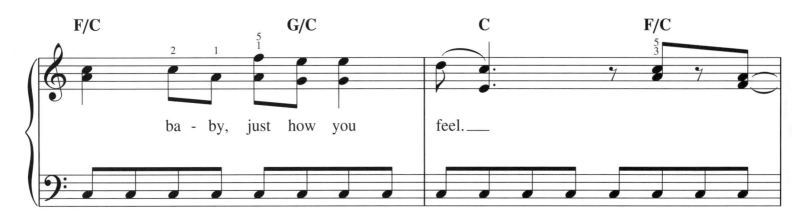

ba - by, just how you feel.___

You got to roll___ with the

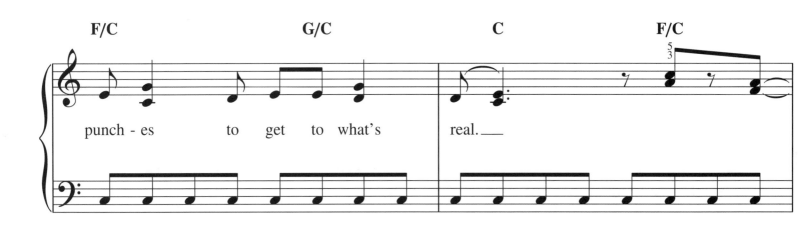

punch - es to get to what's real.___

Ah, can't you see me stand - ing here? I got my

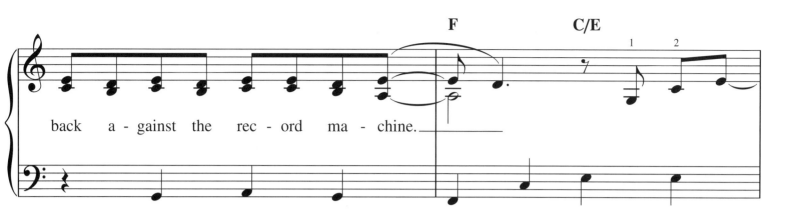

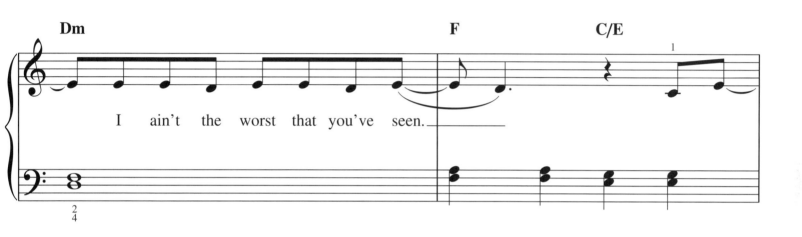

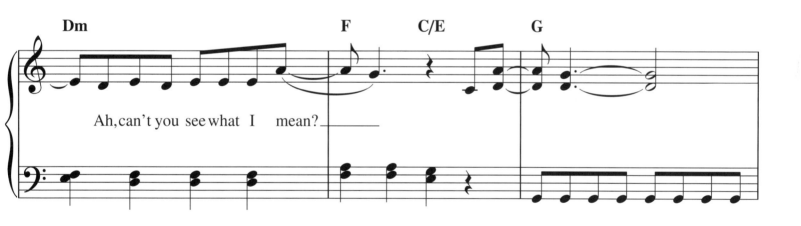

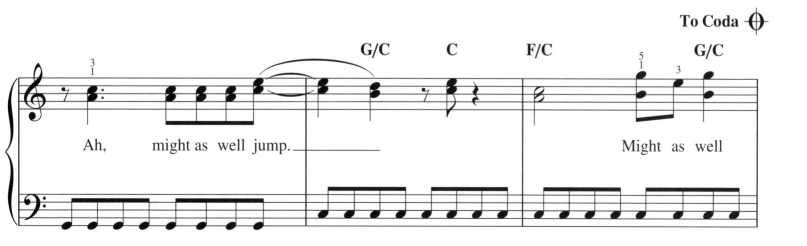

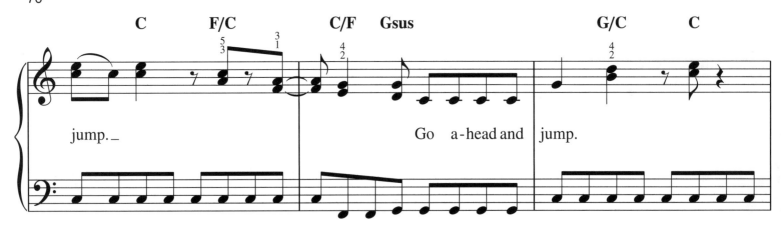

jump. _ Go a-head and jump.

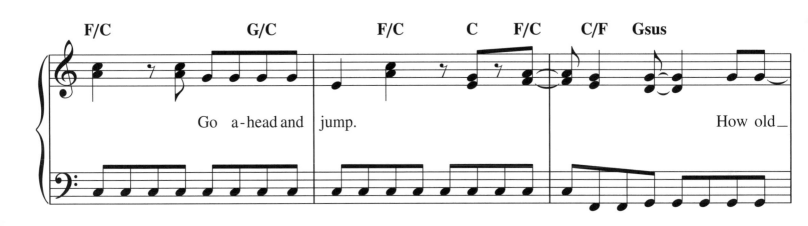

Go a-head and jump. How old _

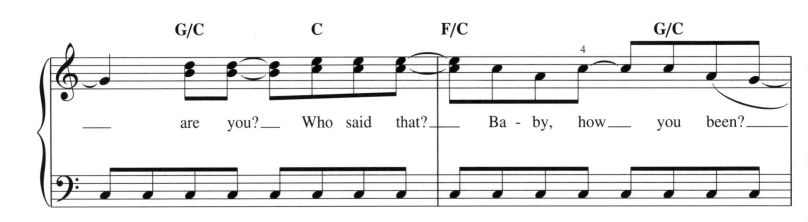

_ are you? _ Who said that? _ Ba - by, how _ you been? _

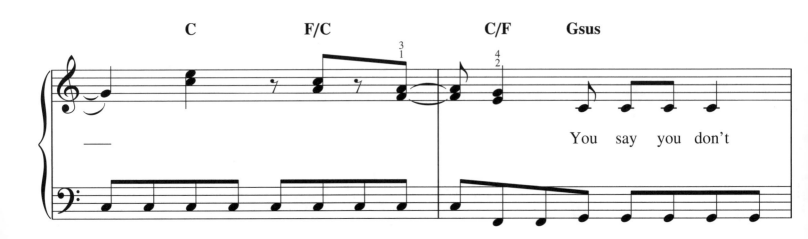

_ You say you don't

know._____ You won't know_ un-til you be - gin._

D.S. al Coda

So can't you

CODA

jump._

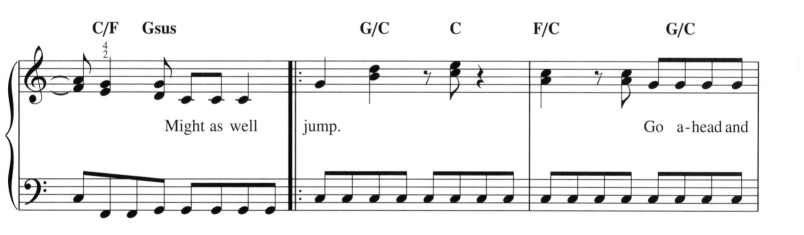

Might as well jump. Go a-head and

jump._ Might as well jump.

TAKE A BOW

Words and Music by SHAFFER SMITH,
TOR ERIK HERMANSEN and MIKKEL ERIKSEN

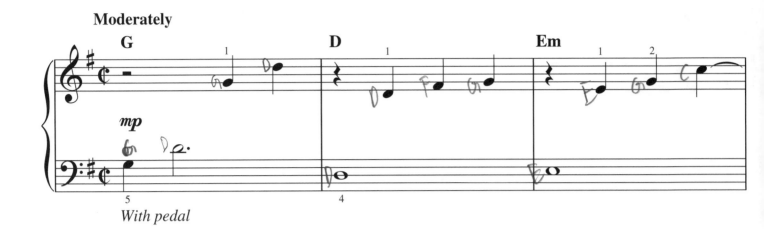

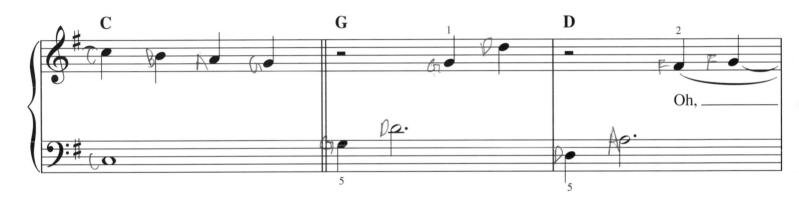

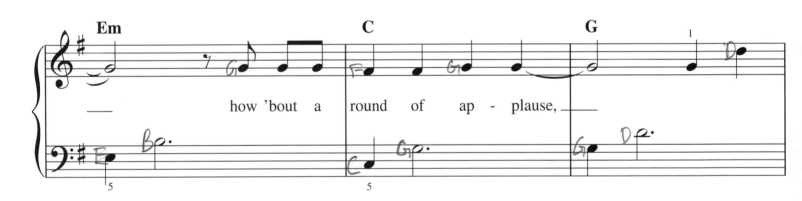

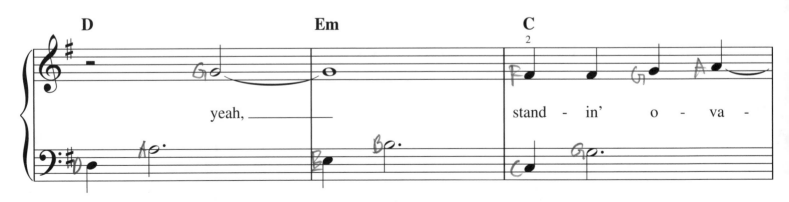

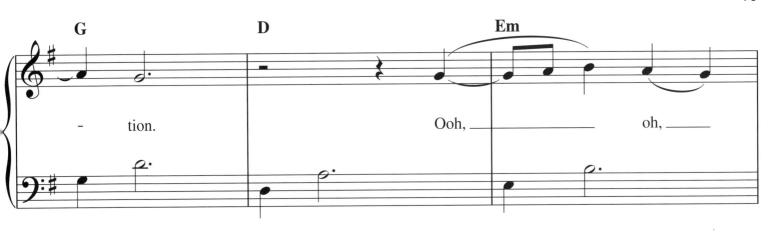

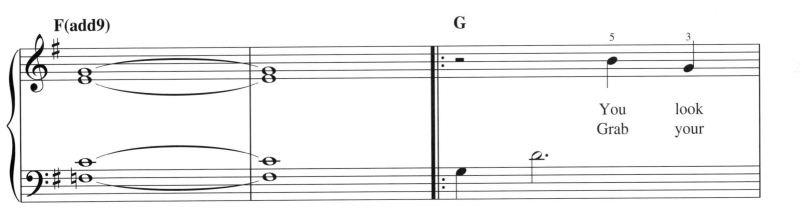

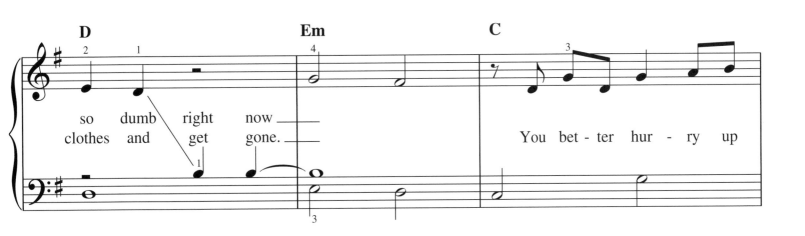

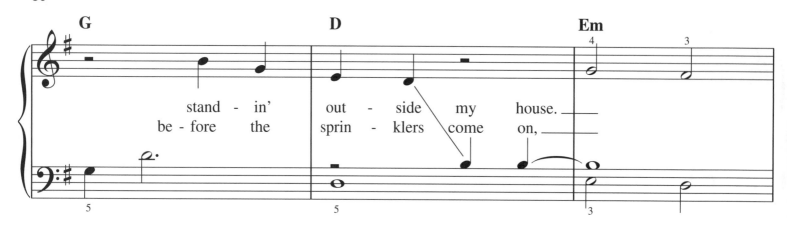

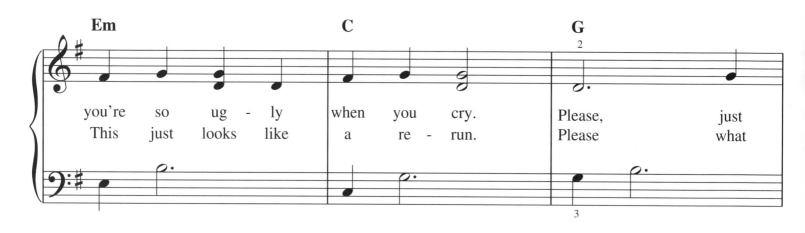

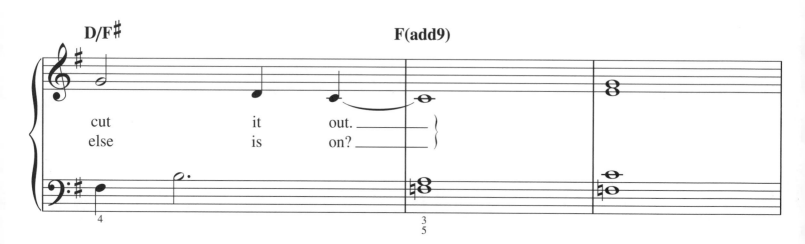

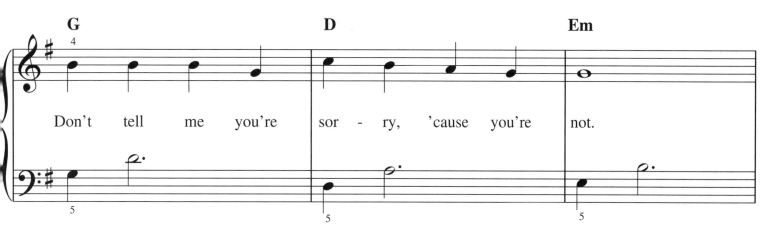

Don't tell me you're sor - ry, 'cause you're not.

And, ba - by, when I know you're on - ly sor - ry you got

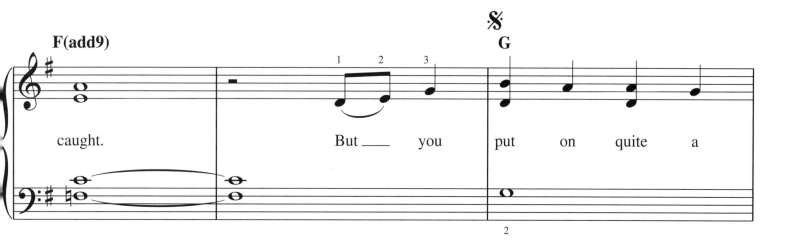

caught. But ___ you put on quite a

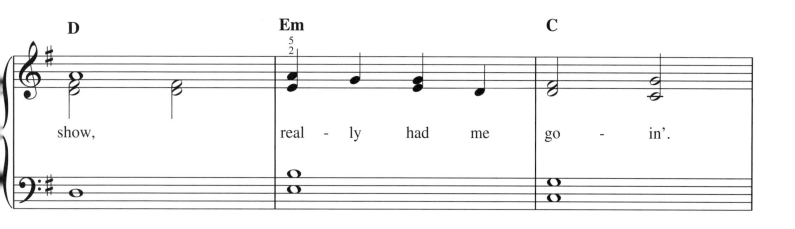

show, real - ly had me go - in'.

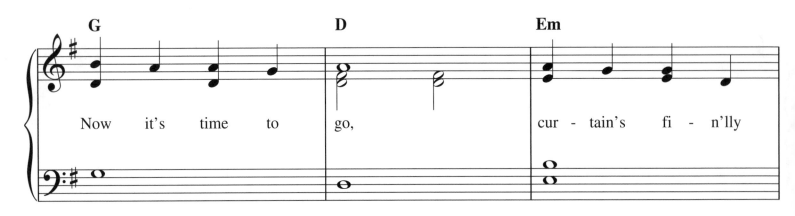

G   **D**   **Em**

Now it's time to go,   cur - tain's fi - n'lly

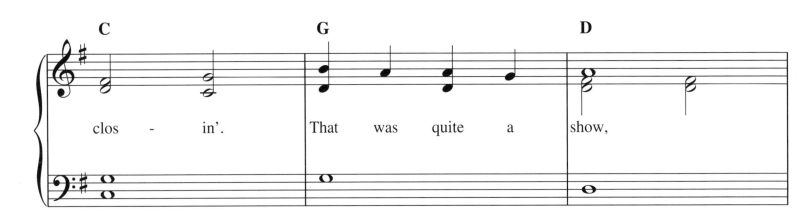

C   **G**   **D**

clos - in'.   That was quite a   show,

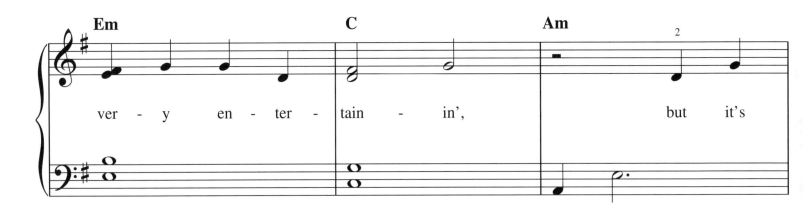

Em   **C**   **Am**

ver - y en - ter - tain - in',   but it's

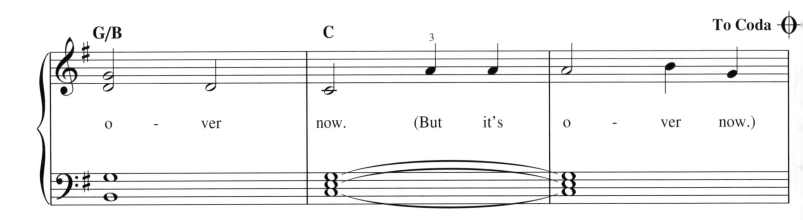

G/B   **C**   **To Coda** ⊕

o - ver   now. (But it's o - ver now.)

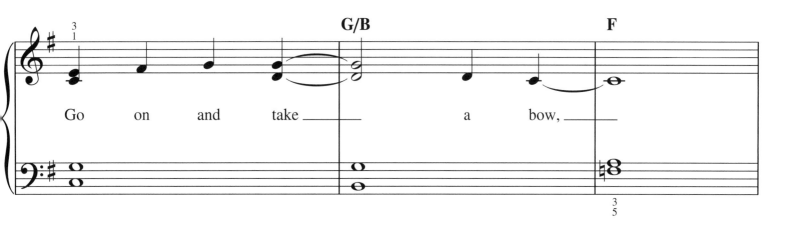

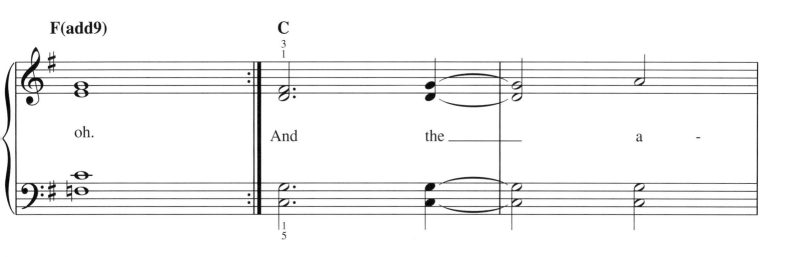

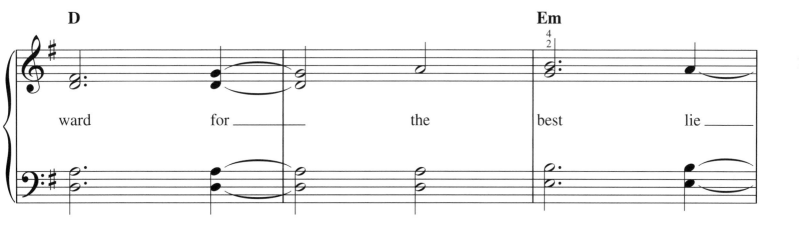

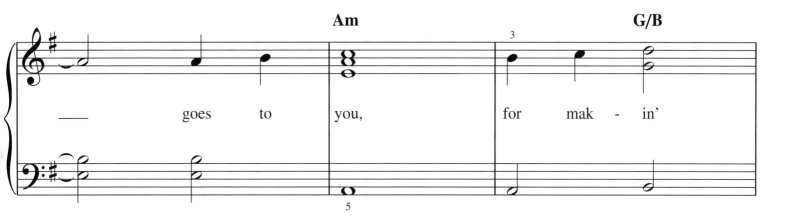

me be - lieve _____ that you could be _____

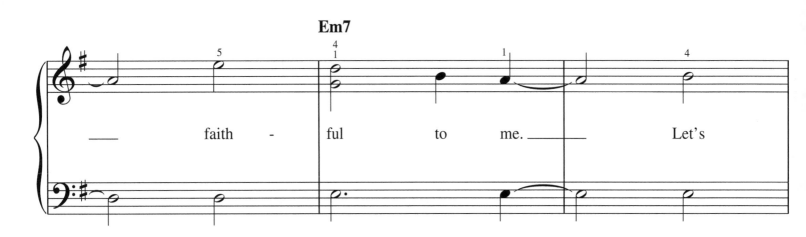

____ faith - ful to me. _____ Let's

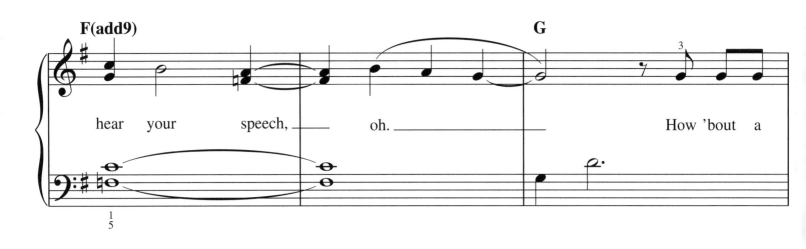

hear your speech, ____ oh. _____ How 'bout a

round of ap - plause, ____

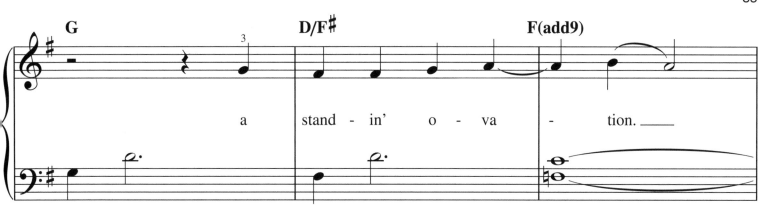

G　**D/F♯**　**F(add9)**

a　stand - in'　o - va - tion. ___

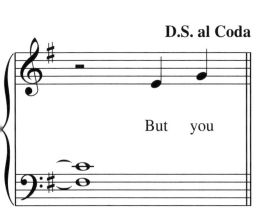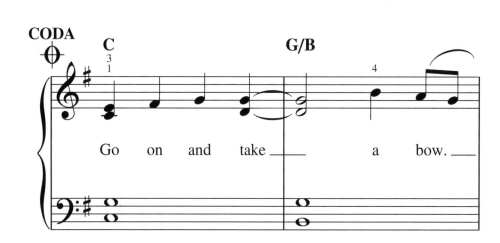

D.S. al Coda

But　you

CODA
C　**G/B**

Go　on　and　take ___　a　bow. ___

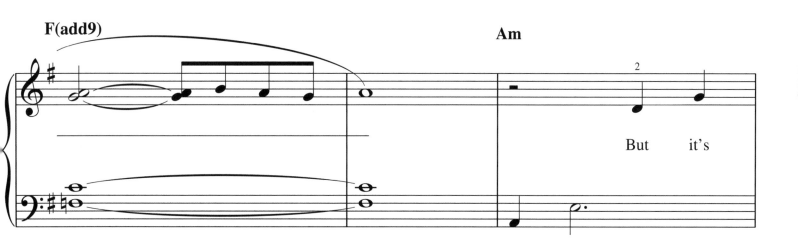

F(add9)　**Am**

But　it's

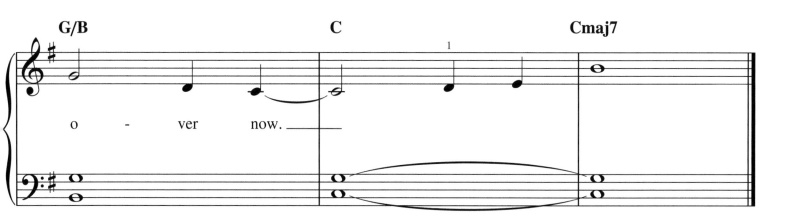

G/B　**C**　**Cmaj7**

o - ver　now. ___

TO SIR, WITH LOVE

from TO SIR, WITH LOVE

Words by DON BLACK
Music by MARC LONDON

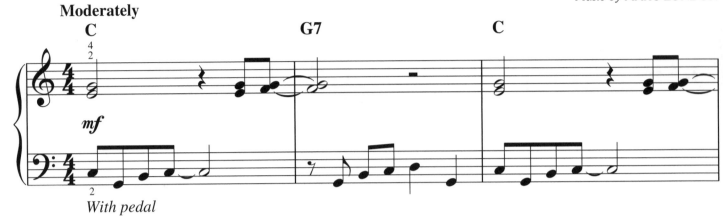

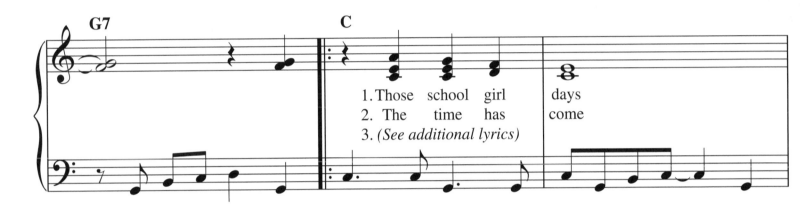

1. Those school girl days
2. The time has come
3. *(See additional lyrics)*

of tell - ing tales and bit - ing nails are gone, ____
for clos - ing books, and long lost looks must end. ____

but in my mind
And as I leave,

I know they will ___ still live on and on. ___
I know that I am leav - ing my best friend, ___

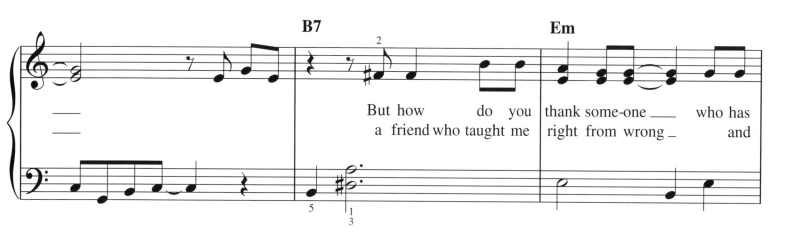

___ But how do you thank some-one ___ who has
___ a friend who taught me right from wrong ___ and

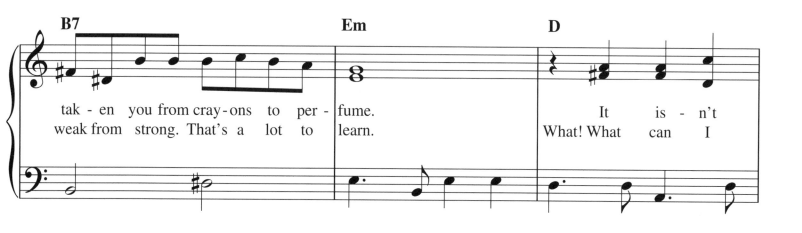

tak - en you from cray-ons to per - fume. It is - n't
weak from strong. That's a lot to learn. What! What can I

eas - y, but I'll try. If you
give you in re - turn? If you

Additional Lyrics

3. Those awkward years have hurried by.
   Why did they fly away?
   Why is it, sir,
   Children grow up to be people one day?
   What takes the place of climbing trees and dirty knees
   In the world outside?
   What is there for you I can buy?
   If you wanted the world,
   I'd surround it with a wall.
   I'd scrawl these words with letters ten feet tall:
   "To sir, with love."